Spiked Helmets of Imperial Germany

SPIKED HELMETS

of

IMPERIAL GERMANY

Infantry Regiments
Pioneer Battalions
General Officers

Wm. Randall Trawnik & Tony Cowan

Schiffer Military History
Atglen, PA

Book Design by Ian Robertson.

Library of Congress Control Number: 2005921418

Printed in China.
ISBN: 0-7643-2168-4

Published by Schiffer Publishing Ltd.
4880 Lower Valley Road
Atglen, PA 19310
Phone: (610) 593-1777
FAX: (610) 593-2002
E-mail: Info@schifferbooks.com.
Visit our web site at: www.schifferbooks.com
Please write for a free catalog.
This book may be purchased from the publisher.
Please include $3.95 postage.
Try your bookstore first.

In Europe, Schiffer books are distributed by:
Bushwood Books
6 Marksbury Avenue
Kew Gardens
Surrey TW9 4JF
England
Phone: 44 (0) 20 8392-8585
FAX: 44 (0) 20 8392-9876
E-mail: info@bushwoodbooks.co.uk.
Free postage in the UK. Europe: air mail at cost.
Try your bookstore first.

Contents

Foreword

Over the years we have met many fellow travelers with whom to enjoy this unusual hobby. For most collectors, the hobby is a mystery due to the lack of reference sources available in the English language. Nearly all of the respected research books related to our hobby have been in French or German. Our collector colleagues Remy Schaal and Walter Hartmann have for years tried to encourage us to write a reference book in English. It is a task not easily undertaken. Several years ago my co-author, Tony Cowan, and I began visiting the great European museums and libraries, and the homes of fellow collectors. This has allowed us to build substantial reference data and photographic base.

At last, at their urging and with the great help of our collector friends we have assembled these books. The first two volumes of *Spiked Helmets of Imperial Germany*—Volume I: Infantry Regiments, Pioneer Battalions, and General Officers, and Volume II: Cavalry, Artillery, and Train—we hope will meet with your approval. As said long ago, "a picture is worth a thousand words." Thus, we hope to present to you complete photographic reference books and text primers for both the beginning and advanced collector.

There were many wonderful people who helped us by sharing their knowledge and research material, as well as allowing us access to their personal collections. A special debt of thanks is owed to the following individuals:

Foreword

To our wives, Marcie Trawnik and Kathy Cowan, for their understanding and encouragement of our unusual hobby.

Remy Schaal, an outstanding friend, for really pushing to get the "ball rolling." He has shared his collection and his constant drive to find new things for our collections.

Walter Hartmann, for sharing his knowledge, contacts, and extensive research materials.

Charles Van Hoenacker, whose collection and knowledge of spiked helmets is without equal. All this he graciously shared with us.

Harry Fakner and his wonderful family for introducing us to his sphere of collectors in Stuttgart.

To the directors and staff members of the Wehrgeschichtliches Museum in Rastatt and the Kavallerie Museum in Vornholz for allowing us access to their collections and wonderful libraries.

To all our many fellow collectors and friends who shared with us their time, photographs, and knowledge. To all of you we wish "good hunting."

Wm. Randall Trawnik
Tony Cowan

To our readers

Ein voellig und einwandfreies Werk ueber Pickelhauben scheint niemanden zu gelingen. Noch sind immer Fehler zu berichtigen und Luecken zu fuellen. Vielen Dank fuer euer verstandnis.

A complete and absolutely correct study of spiked helmets is impossible to do. There will always be corrections to be made and holes to fill. Many thanks for your understanding.

Presentation of Regimental Schellenbaums circa 1900.

1

The Story of the German Spiked Helmet

Brunswick Officer Helmet

Grand Duchies
Baden
Hessen-Darmstadt
Oldenburg
Mecklenburg-Schwerin
Mecklenburg-Strelitz
Saxe-Weimar-Eisenach

Kingdoms
Prussia
Bavaria
Saxony
Wuerttemberg

Free Cities
Hamburg
Bremen
Luebeck

Principalities
Lippe
Reuss
Waldeck
Schaumberg-Lippe
Schwarzburg-Rudolstadt
Schwarzburg-Sonderhausen

Duchies
Anhalt
Braunschweig
Saxe-Altenburg
Saxe-Coburg-Gotha
Saxe-Meiningen
Nassau

Map of Germany 1870

Perhaps no piece of military headgear more exemplifies a nation or an age than the "Pickelhaube," or spiked helmet. The original helmet design adopted by the Kingdom of Prussia in 1842 eventually became the standard headgear for the Imperial German Army.

The era of the "**Pickelhaube**" corresponded with the building of the German nation. The history of Germany is, in actuality, the study of many different kingdoms, principalities, and city-states, bound together by a common language and cultural heritage. The Kingdom of Prussia had a rich military history and traditions dating back to the era of Frederick the Great. Under the able political leadership of Prime Minster Otto von Bismarck and the fine Army lead by Generals like von Molke, Prussia was the natural leader of the north German states.

Military fashion of the early 1800s was dominated by the design of Napoleon Bonaparte. Nearly all the armies of Europe copied the tall shako used by the French and their allies. During the Napoleonic era, Prussia developed a tall leather and felt shako after the French pattern. Besides its awkward shape, the chief complaint was its weight and instability when wet. By the 1840s many European countries sought to develop their own unique military fashions.

The origin of the spiked helmet is shrouded in the fog of history. A popular story states that in 1840 the Prussian King Frederick Wilhelm IV, while visiting his brother-in-law Czar Nicholas I of Russia, happened to see the prototype for a new helmet on the Czar's desk. The helmet was made of black leather and ornamented with a tall flowered spike on the top of the helmet. This helmet was supposedly patterned after an ancient helmet found by a Russian farm girl on the old battlefield of Lipezk. The helmet was said to have belonged to Jaroslav Vaevolodovitch, the famous 12th century Duke of Moscow. King Frederick was so taken with the helmet that, upon returning home to Prussia, he demanded that his army design their own version of the spiked helmet.

The Prussian War Ministry immediately began seeking designs for the new helmet. By March 1841 the Metallwarenfabrik Wilhelm Jaeger of Eberfeld presented the prototype spiked helmet to the army. The new helmet, designed for use by the mounted kurassiers, was made of metal. Field trials were very complimentary of the size, weight, protection, and versatility of the new helmet style. Cavalry commander General von Brautisch wrote:

1. The prototype helmet without plume was lighter than the presently used helmet.
2. The helmet looks good and has a lower profile than the present helmet.
3. The helmet sat comfortably on the head and did not become dislodged by the trooper's movements.
4. The helmet wears well in heavy winds and bad weather.
5. The trooper's head is better protected with the new helmet.
6. The front visor of the helmet allows the wearer to aim and fire his weapon while having the practical aspect of shading the eyes from the light.
7. The design and construction of the back visor of the helmet is very practical. The form protects the neck but does not rub the uniform collar.
8. The leather liner is open above the head to reduce the build up of heat inside the helmet.
9. The helmet design allows it to be quickly removed by the wearer.
10. Aesthetically, the new helmet is far superior to the older pattern helmet.

The War Ministry immediately began serious development of the helmet design. The "Pickelhaube" (German for spiked head covering) helmet became the standard Prussian headdress. Quickly, other branches of the German Army also designed helmets for use. Although the first prototype was made of metal for the kurassiers, it was the leather pattern helmet designed for the infantry and artillery that was first put into use. By late 1842 the Prussian War Ministry and the Quartermaster accepted the spiked helmet for use. The original metal designed spiked helmet was adopted for use by the kurassiers in 1843.

Prussian Officers circa 1845

The **Model 1842** spiked helmet was made of leather for use by regiments of infantry, grenadier, fusilier, artillery, pioneer, dragoons, and jäger (who later changed to the shako). The helmet body was made of heavy vegetable tanned and pressed leather. The body was conical in shape and sewn together in the back. The front visor was square cut and edged with a 1 cm wide metal trim. The back visor was plain leather. All exterior leather was lacquered black. The helmet was crowned with a 14 cm tall spike mounted in the middle of a crossed base. The sewn area at the back of the helmet body was crested by a metal ridge or spine. The back spine extended from the edge of the spike base to the back edge of the rear visor. The chinstrap was made of vegetable tanned sheepskin and covered with rounded metal scales. The chinscales were affixed to the helmet body with an ornate knurled screw through an elongated rosette. Under the right rosette was placed a black and white colored cockade. The cockade was made of lacquered leather for enlisted men, while officers wore leather mounted with a silver ring. The front emblem for "Regiments of the Line" was the Prussian heraldic eagle. Guard Regiments wore a spread-winged eagle with the silver star of the Black Eagle Order on the eagle's breast. Grenadier regiments wore the heraldic eagle with the intertwined royal monogram **FWR** on the eagle's breast.

The spiked top helmet was quickly copied or adopted by many of the independent states allied with Prussia. By the late 1860s all but the independent kingdoms of Saxony, Wuerttemberg, and Bavaria looked to Prussia for military leadership. The Military Convention of 1867 formed the basis for a unified German national army. This alliance insured mutual cooperation and protection to the allied German states. At that time most of the states adopted the Prussian style dress and spiked helmet. The victory over the French in the Franco-Prussian War (1870-71) initiated the formation of the 2nd Kaiserreich (Empire), with the Prussian King Wilhelm I as its emperor. The Military convention of 1871 formalized the establishment of the unified Imperial Army. By 1886 all German states had adopted the Prussian style "pickelhaube."

Prior to World War I, the important style changes in the evolution of the spiked helmet were:

1842: Introduction of the spiked helmet.
1844: Introduction of the "ball" finial for artillery regiments.
1857: Reduction in overall size and weight of helmet (2 cm shorter).
1860: Significant reduction in size of helmet (4cm). Spike and base also reduced in size.
1867: Radically different helmet design. Front visor now has round metal edging, with the spike base also being round. The back spine is completely eliminated.
1871: Due to the instability of the 1867 design, the back spine is returned on the helmet.
1887: New style helmet for enlisted model helmet. Metal front visor trim removed and replaced with a hardened curled leather edge. Chinscale rosettes are replaced with a hook retention system. Pearl ring at spike base is removed. Many older pattern helmets are refitted with the new chinstrap. Some units are not required to wear the new model at all. Thus there are a number of variations of this model helmet. Officers continue to wear the Model 1871 helmet.*
1891: Change in style for the enlisted model helmet. The metal front visor trim reintroduced. M-87 chinscale hooks are replaced with lug retainer (M91 side lug) for a scaled or leather type of chinstrap.
1895: Reduction in size and weight of helmet (body now 12.5 cm tall). Back spine for enlisted pattern helmets of foot troops was fitted with a ventilation sleeve (Mounted troops received the vented back spine in 1904). **This helmet model was worn by enlisted troops at the outbreak of WWI.**
1897: Introduction of the black/white/red Reichs cockade to be worn in conjunction with the state cockade.
1915: Modification to the M1895 enlisted pattern helmet. Introduction of matte gray oxidized steel to replace bright metal trim. Spike also made to be removable at base by a bayonet lock mechanism.

Please see Appendix C for a more complete listing of regulations that affected the development of the spiked helmet.

**The Model 1871 will be retained as the model Officer helmet until World War I. The helmet will change by becoming lighter in weight and more elegant in construction but otherwise remains the same.*

Prussian Guard Officer to Parade – Mod. 1842

Model 1842

Model 1857 – Cut Down Mod. 1842

Model 1860

Model 1867

Model 1871: 91st Oldenburg Infantry Enlisted Man

Model 1887: Saxon Infantry Regiments

Model 1891-95

Model 1915

The "Pickelhaube" became such a popular headdress in the late 1890s that many countries adopted their own version of the spiked helmet. Those countries include Sweden, Norway, Rumania, Denmark, Spain, Portugal, Great Britain, Brazil, Chile, Equator, Peru, Mexico, Duchy of Parma, and the United States.

Officer's helmet from Mexico circa 1910

Spiked Helmets of the Pre-WWI Era

Kaiser Wilhelm II dearly loved the pomp and ceremony associated with his great army. His interest in military fashion helped develop the spiked helmet into an art form by the turn of the century. Colorful uniforms and elaborate parades gave the German public pride in their national army. During this time many elite regiments received special helmet banners to glorify their rich history or feats of valor. The helmet itself became lighter and the metal trim more elaborate. Young officers competed on who could have the tallest spike.

The richness of German military tradition, the variety of helmet styles, and also the added availability of helmets in the market place has helped to increase the number of spiked helmet collectors. The helmets of the pre-war period and those used during World War I remain the most popular among collectors today.

Saxon NCO circa 1910

Helmet Identification

Please note that there is naturally a remarkable quality difference from private purchase helmets versus the standard issue model. All officers, one-year volunteers, faehnrichs (officer candidates), and many non-commissioned officers were required to purchase their helmets from private manufacturers. Enlisted pattern helmets were issued by the army and were mass-produced.

Authors note: The information provided below is designed as an overview of the subject. Space limitations make extensive study of the subject impossible in this article. Please contact the authors with any specific questions or comments related to individual helmets.

Helmet Body

There are three basic body styles used by spiked helmets of the post-1890 era. The authors have termed the styles as:

STANDARD: Round front visor and round spike base

DRAGOON: Square front visor and crossed spike base

HESSEN: Round front visor and equal armed spike base

STANDARD STYLE | DRAGOON STYLE | HESSEN STYLE

Helmet Body Models

All military helmets use these pattern helmet bodies *except* Saxon General Officers and some Wuerttemberg NCO/I Year Volunteers, which may have squared front visors and round spike bases. ***Many non-military, fire, civil servant, and police units wore spiked helmets similar to the military helmets. They use different body/trim criteria than the military pieces***. Do not confuse them with military helmets.

The helmet bell was conical in shape and made of pressed leather. Officers' helmets were made of thinner leather and were sewn together in the rear under the back spine. Issue helmets were made of thicker leather, and were usually formed out of one piece of leather without being sewn in the back. The front and back visors were sewn to the helmet body, with the front visor edged with metal trim. All exterior leather was black lacquered. Officer quality helmets were lighter and more finely stitched than issue quality helmets. Issue helmets were mounted with M91 side lugs on each side of the helmet for the retention of the chinstrap (Mod. 1915 officer helmets also used the M91 side lug, over which was placed a special slotted faux rosette and chinscaled strap).* Officer chinscales were affixed to the helmet body through holes in the sides, and held in place with a split braid rosette. The front plate was attached to the enlisted helmet through two grommet-lined holes in the front of the helmet body. Officer helmets merely had two small, unlined holes through the body to mount the front plate.

The interior of the officer helmet featured a fine serrated edge lambskin leather sweatband topped with a ribbed *ottoman* silk headliner (**Officer helmets of the Pre 1880 era did use leather liners). Issue helmets had a leather "tongue style" liner. The liner was held together with a retention cord that passed through a hole in each tongue. The inner visors of officer helmets were lined with colored paper or leather. The colors were usually (but not always) green under the front and red under the back visor. Officer model back visors also had a sewn fancy leather edging. Issue helmets had plain leather inner visors that usually had regimental or quartermaster corps inked stamps. It is important to the collector to make sure the regimental markings properly match with the helmet front plate.

Metal Trim

The front plate (Helmzier) is the most important element of the spiked helmet. Troops of the different German States were able to show regional patriotism with their own heraldic crest. In addition to state distinctions, elite and historical regiments outfitted their crest with special banners. There were over 30 front plates for regiments of foot (infantry, grenadiers, etc) alone. This diversity makes collecting interesting and challenging.

Victory pyramid of spiked helmets exhibited in Central Park, New York City, 1919.

FRONTPLATES

PRUSSIA

1.
2, 3, & 4 G. R. zu Foot
1 - 5 Guard Grenadier Regt.s

2.
1st Guard of Foot 1st Bat.

3.
1st G.R.zu F. II-III Bat
Guard Fusilier - 5th G.R. zu F.

4a.
1st Gren. Regt. Pre-1900

4b.
1st Grenadier Regt. Post-1900

5a.
Gren. Regt. 4 Pre-1911

5b.
Grenadier Regt. 4 Post-1911

6.
Grenadier Regt. 7

7a.
Gren. Regt. 9 Pre-1913

7b
Gren. Regt. 9 Post-1913

8a.
Gren. R. 2,3,8 - 145 / 5,6,10,11,12
Post 1912

8b.
Gren. R. 5,6,10,11-12 Pre 1912

9.
Prussian Regiments of the Line **
LIST OF REGIMENTS NEXT PAGE

10.
Fus. Regt. 33 5-6 Comp.
Fusilier Regt. 34

11.
Fusiler Regt. 73

12.
Inf. Regt. 74,77,78, 164 & 165

13.
Infantry Regt. 87

14.
Infantry Regt. 88

MECKLENBURG STRELITZ

15.
Grenadier Regt.89 I Bat.

MECK SCHWERIN

16.
Gren. Regt. 89 I-III Bat
Fusilier Regt. 90

OLDENBURG

17.
Infantry Regt. 91

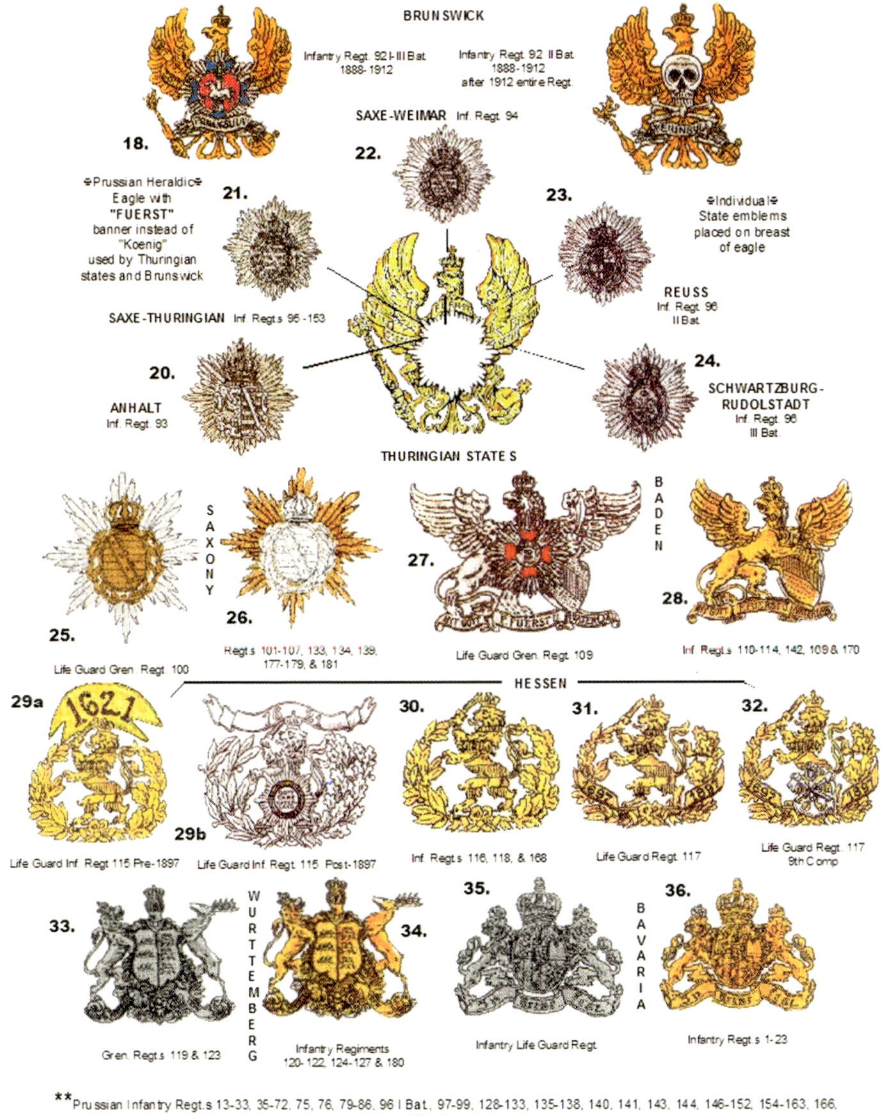

**Prussian Infantry Regt.s 13-33, 35-72, 75, 76, 79-86, 96 I Bat., 97-99, 128-133, 135-138, 140, 141, 143, 144, 146-152, 154-163, 166, 167, 171-176.

Above and opposite: Front Plates of the Infantry 1914

GERMAN REICH

PRUSSIA

ANHALT

BRAUNSCHWEIG

SCHWARZBURG-RUD.

LIPPE DETMOLD

SAXE-WEIMAR

MECKLENBURG

OLDENBURG

REUSS & WALDECK

HAMBURG & LUBECK

✠Hamburg has flat area atop cross

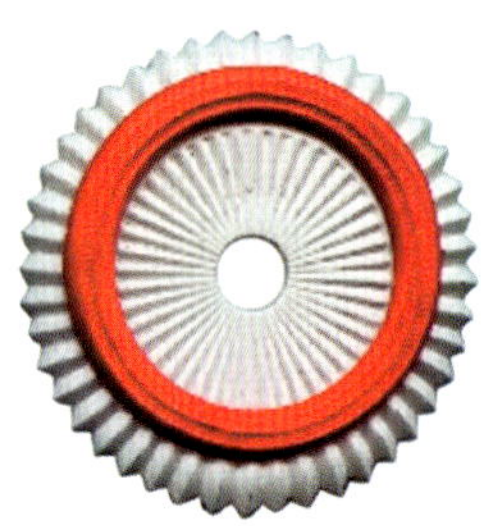

BREMEN

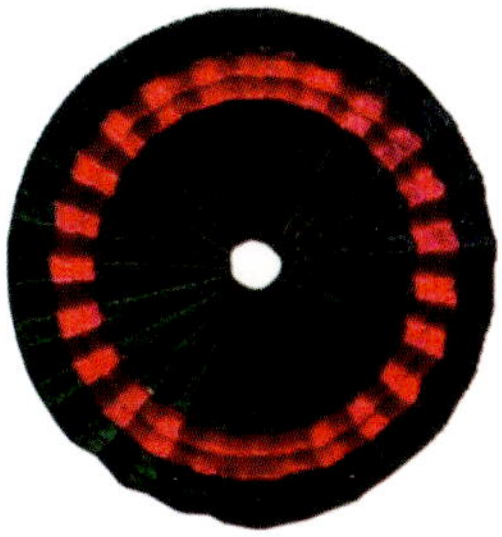
WUERTTEMBERG

WUERTTEMBERG M15

BAVARIA

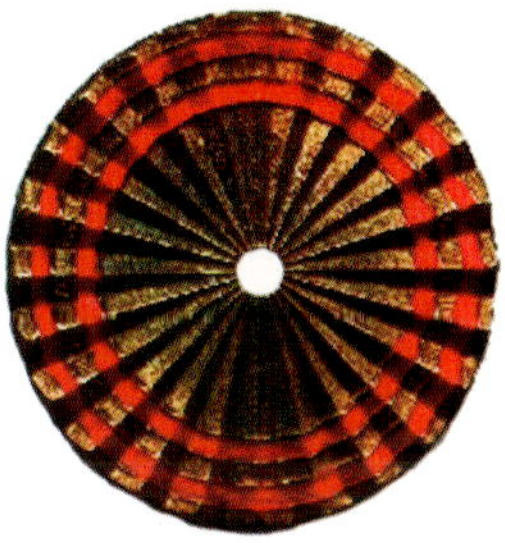
BADEN

BADEN M15

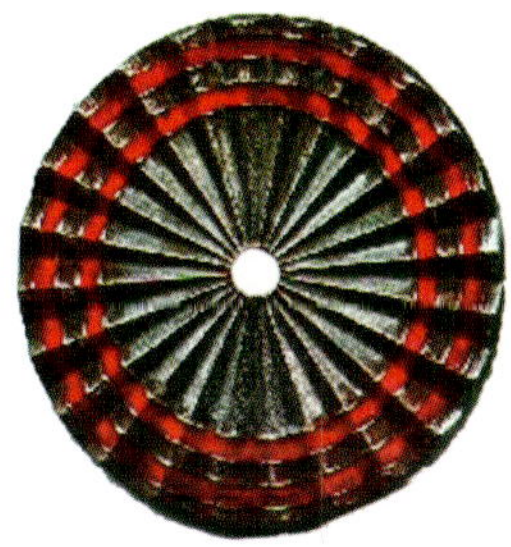
HESSEN

SCHAUMBURG-LIPPE

SONDERHAUSEN

SAXON-THURINGEN

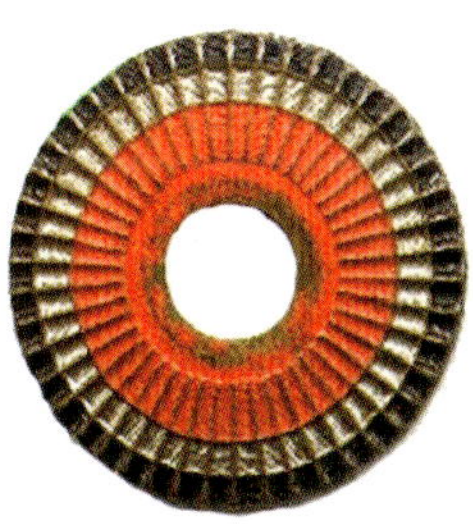

Officer Helmet Cockades

In addition to the front plate, metal trim for the spiked helmet included front visor trim, base-spike unit, plume trichters (mounts) for parade, spike base retainers, back spine, chinstrap with M91 mount and chinscales with rosette or leather chinstrap, and enameled cockades. All trim was made of stamped (not cast) brass, german silver, or tombak (for Guards Regt.s). Issue quality trim was highly polished and usually lacquered. Officers' trim, especially front plates, were fire gilded (or frosted, in the case of silver front plates).

The cockades were mounted behind the chinstrap or chinscale. The red/white/black REICHS cockade, introduced in 1897, was on the right side of the helmet. The NATIONAL cockade displayed the distinct state colors and was mounted on the left side of the helmet. Cockades exhibited several forms and contours depending on the state, rank, and manufacture date. Officer style cockades were usually made in two pieces and approximately 6.5 cm. Cockades for enlisted troops were flat stamped and enameled with a diameter of 4.5 cm.

Special distinctions separate the quality and appearance of metal trim used on officer/private purchase versus issued helmets. They include:

	Officer	***Issue Helmet***
Front plate	Fine detail, voided crown on top of emblem. Retained to helmet body with threaded bolt and nut. Fire gilded. Special units that wore "star" distinctions were multi-piece constructed with enameled centers.	Inferior quality stamping than officer. Crown closed. Retained to helmet body with loops and leather wedge. Polished facade. Special units that wore "star" distinctions were one piece stamped.
Visor Trim:	Visor trim approx. .6 cm wide.	Visor trim approx. 1 cm wide.
Spike/Base	Officer has higher profile with "pearl and diamond" ornamentation at base.* Eight pointed star retainers to affix base to helmet body.*	Simple design with no pearl ring at spike base. Base affixed to helmet body with domed split leg retainers.

Trichter: Plume	Formed like an elongated spike and approx . 12 cm tall. After 1896 the plume is made of buffalo hair.	Formed like a tube extending from top of the base and approx. 10 cm tall. Plume made of horse hair.
Back Spine	Spine ribbed along edge.*	Spine has a ventilation hole with movable cover.*
Chinstrap	Chinscales with push through rosette. Flat scales for troops of foot. Rounded for mounted troops.*	Leather chinstrap on M91 lug. Some units wore M91 mounted chinscales for parade or guard duty. Flat/Rounded like officer.
Cockades	**Usually 2 piece construction.** (several exceptions)	**Flat stamped and enameled.**

**excluding Hessen pattern helmets.*

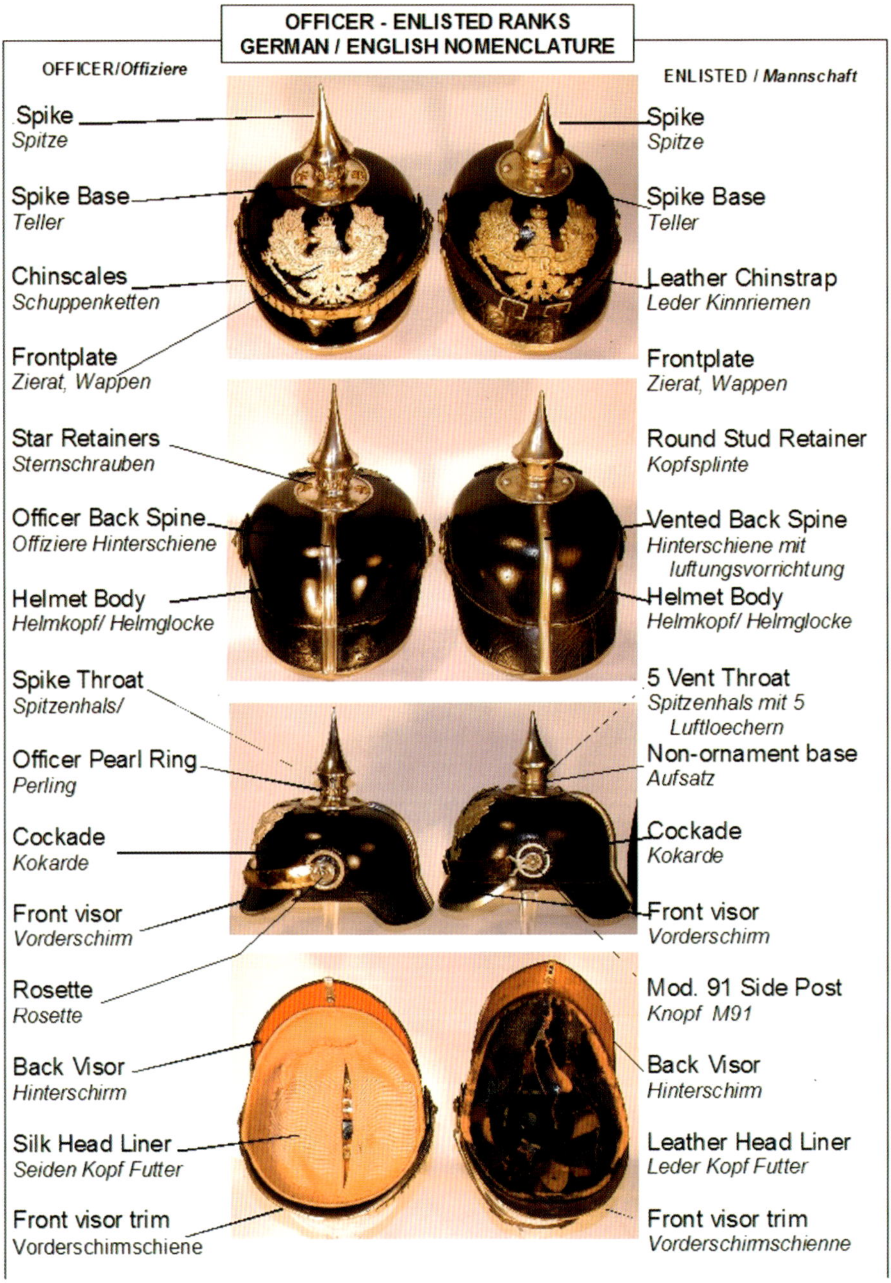
OFFICER - ENLISTED RANKS
GERMAN / ENGLISH NOMENCLATURE
OFFICER/Offiziere
ENLISTED / Mannschaft
Spike
Spitze
Spike Base
Teller
Chinscales
Schuppenketten
Leather Chinstrap
Leder Kinnriemen
Frontplate
Zierat, Wappen
Star Retainers
Sternschrauben
Round Stud Retainer
Kopfsplinte
Officer Back Spine
Offiziere Hinterschiene
Vented Back Spine
Hinterschiene mit luftungsvorrichtung
Helmet Body
Helmkopf/ Helmglocke
Spike Throat
Spitzenhals/
5 Vent Throat
Spitzenhals mit 5 Luftloechern
Officer Pearl Ring
Perling
Non-ornament base
Aufsatz
Cockade
Kokarde
Front visor
Vorderschirm
Rosette
Rosette
Mod. 91 Side Post
Knopf M91
Back Visor
Hinterschirm
Silk Head Liner
Seiden Kopf Futter
Leather Head Liner
Leder Kopf Futter
Front visor trim
Vorderschirmschiene
Vorderschirmschienne

OFFICER - OTHER RANKS COMPARISON CHART

OFFICER

FRONTPLATE: Fine detail with voided crown on top of the emblem. Retained to helmet body with threaded bolt/nut. Fire gilded or silver frosted. Special units with "star" distinction were multi-piece with enamelled centers.
VISOR TRIM: approx. .6 cm wide.
HELMET BODY: Conical shaped pressed leather finely sewn in the back under the rear metal spine
REAR SPINE: Single piece extending from the spike base around edge of back visor. Spine ribbed in contour.**
SPIKE/BASE: Spike is taller than EM pattern. Unit has "pearl - diamond" ornamentation at base. Eight pointed star retainers affix unit to helmet body.**
CHINSTRAP: Scaled chin strap secured to body with push through rosette. Flat scales for troops of foot. Rounded scales for mounted troops. ** All chinscales gold colored except 1 GRzF, 100 LGR, 115 LGIR. All Bavarian units have chinscales to match trim color.
ROSETTES: Metal color of rosette match trim color. (i.e. Silver trimmed helmet will have silver rosette and gold scales.

COCKADES: Usually 2 piece construction. 6.5 cm diameter.

INSIDE LINER: Soft sweat leather band with Ottoman silk headliner split in middle. Inner visors red material back and green lined in front.

ENLISTED

FRONTPLATE: Stamped brass or german silver. Crown closed. Retained to the helmet body with 2 metal loops and leather wedges. Polished façade. Special units that wore "star" distinctions were simply stamped out of silver colored metal.
VISOR TRIM: approx. 1 cm. wide.
HELMET BODY: Made of thicker leather formed out of one piece of leather without being sewn in the back.
REAR SPINE: Spine extends from under spike base around edge of back visor. Ventilation hole with moveable cover. **
SPIKE/BASE: Simple spike design with no pearl ring at spike base. Base affixed to helmet body with domed split leg retainers. ✠NCO and ✠One Year Volunteer can have pearl ring.
CHINSTRAP: Adjustable leather chinstrap that fits over M91 side lug. Metal fittings match the trim of the helmet. NCO and some unit EM wear chinscales for parade or guard duty. Flat for troops of foot and rounded for mounted troops. Color of chinscales match that used by officer units
ROSETTE/SIDE LUG: Metal color to match color of other trim. NCO and 1 Year Volunteer to match style used by officer.
COCKADES: EM and 1 Year Volunteer stamped single piece. NCO can have 2 piece construction. 4.5 cm diameter.
INSIDE LINER: Sturdy black or natural colored leather drawstring liner. Inside visors natural color. Usually stamped with Regt. marks.

✠NCO-1 Yr. Vol. Helmets were not issued but purchased by wearer.

** HESSEN HELMETS EXCEPTION TO THIS RULE -

Spiked Helmets of World War I

The German soldiers went to war in 1914 wearing the Model 1895 leather spiked helmet. All the bright metal trim was hidden by a gray/green cloth field cover. After the initial push into France, the German High Command realized that more men were needed to achieve the victory over the Allies. Many thousands of helmets were fabricated early in the war to meet the needs expressed by the army quartermasters. Quickly, the extreme demand and reduction of available raw materials led to the use of replacement materials. Leather, in short supplies due to the allied sea embargo, left many helmet manufacturers without the ability to meet their army contracts for helmets. To meet this demand pressed felt, paper Maché, synthetic fiber, cork, and stamped tin replaced the leather helmet body in many war model **ersatz** helmets.

The need for brass, which was used for shell casings, was acute. It was quickly clear to the German High Command that the spiked helmet was impractical for use in the trenches. The final helmet design change (**Model 1915**) replaced the bright metal trim with matte gray painted or chemically oxidized steel trim for all issue helmets. The unique element of the **Mod.15** was the ability to remove the entire spike at the base by use of a bayonet lock mechanism. This reduced the profile of the helmet and made it better for use in trench warfare. Manufacturers of officer helmets also adopted some of the Model 1915 changes. Officer spikes were made to be removable at the base, and Mod. 91 style side lugs were used to allow officers to remove chinscales in the field and replace them with a more practical leather chinstrap.

The "Pickelhaube" was designed and created in a time of colorful uniforms, great parades, and grand illusions. Sadly, it served the German soldier poorly in the time of high velocity shells and savage trench warfare. The troops in the field required more protection than the leather helmet could offer. In early 1916 the "coal scuttle" steel helmet was introduced to the front line soldiers. Almost immediately the spiked helmet disappeared from active use in the trenches. The spiked helmet continued to find use among rear echelon and home based troops. Many officers refused to give up the symbol of the old army and continued to wear the helmet until war's end.

German Soldier circa 1914

Bavarian Felt Ersatz Helmet

German Soldier circa 1917

Guidelines for the Modern Collector

Collecting militaria is likened to going on a treasure hunt. Collectors are always looking for the "find" that will bring us joy and add a "piece of history" to our collections. Fortunately for "Pickelhaube" collectors, there were many thousands of helmets brought home as souvenirs after the war. Immediately following the war the U.S. Army occupied Koblenz. There they found over 20,000 unissued spiked helmets. These helmets were sent to the U.S. and given away to purchasers of the Bonds for the War Loan Drive of 1919. After World War II the spiked helmet was again a popular souvenir for the American soldier and later tourists. Thus, helmets still surface at estate sales, flea markets, and gun shows. The rapid approach of the Centennial of the "Great War" has also attracted the attention of the collecting public. Thus helmet values are increasing, and the availability of helmets in the market place is beginning to shrink.

Although the hobby is large and gaining new collectors daily, there has been very little in the way of reference and research material available in the English language concerning the study of the German Spiked Helmet. To determine the value of an individual helmet the purchaser must be **knowledgeable** about helmet design and construction, and be able to identify the front plates of the German states and regiments.

German Helmets Arrive in New York Warehouse 1919

Captured German Helmets as Liberty Loan Prizes

When the Yanks entered Coblenz they captured a large quantity of German helmets. We have secured a quantity of them for distribution as prizes to your most conspicuously successful Liberty Loan workers during the Victory Liberty Loan Drive.

These helmets were intended to be issued to the German Army to be worn in their triumphant entrance into the City of Paris.

Each local chairman should feel at liberty to use the helmets sent him to stimulate the sales of the Victory Liberty Loan in the greatest degree. He need not feel obliged to follow the plan which we outline below.

In cities three helmets have been allotted to each ward, and it is recommended that the local chairman consider giving on each of the three Saturday nights in the Campaign, at some hour to be determined by himself, one of the helmets as a prize to the person who has secured during the week the largest number of individual subscriptions to the Loan on which the first payment has actually been made. This will institute a sales contest, which will be fresh each week and last during the entire Loan, and should greatly stimulate the distribution of Victory Notes among the people. Be sure, please, that all subscriptions are bona fide.

To each town two helmets have been allotted. We recommend that one helmet be awarded as a prize to the person who has secured during the week the largest number of individual subscriptions to the Loan, on which the first payment has actually been made. We recommend the other helmet be given to the person who brings in subscriptions amounting to the largest volume in dollars. It is possible that both helmets would go to the same person.

Publicity has been prepared and sent out to all the local newspapers, and the distribution of these helmets will prove to be one of the most interesting features of the Campaign.

We recommend that additional publicity be secured in the local papers and that the helmets be exhibited in the most prominent store, or bank, windows, with signs attached showing the conditions upon which the local chairmen finally decides they will distribute.

Don't hesitate to push this feature to the limit. It will prove a great assistance in getting proper distribution for this Loan.

Yours for the "Victory" Liberty Loan,

LIBERTY LOAN COMMITTEE OF NEW ENGLAND,

JOHN K. ALLEN,

Chairman, Publicity Committee.

95 MILK STREET, BOSTON, MASS.

War Loan Circular 1919

When considering a piece for purchase the important considerations are **originality**, **rank**, **condition**, and **rarity.** When evaluating a helmet for purchase one should use keen observation and common sense. Our criteria includes:

1. In order to be **original**, all metal parts should have been attached to the helmet since its manufacture. The metal trim should match in color and configure snugly to the contour of the helmet. The helmet was originally designed for an 18-year use life by the army. Many helmets were altered during the time of use by the quartermaster or by officers who purchased used helmets in order to save money. It is also not uncommon to find wartime issued helmets that have mismatched parts. In the years since WWI some helmets have lost parts and pieces due to neglect and aging. Due to this some helmets require "restoration" with the replacement of a missing part. This should be done carefully and using original period parts when available. The replacement of a missing part will improve the appearance and value of the helmet, but an unaltered helmet will still have a greater value. As a collector, I am not opposed to restoring a helmet to its original station. *We do oppose altering a helmet from its original use or rank*. The collector must check to make sure that the front plate of a "rare" unit helmet has not been added at a later date. Everything from rare front plates, metal back spines, and even leather helmet bodies are now being reproduced. The collector should be on the lookout for helmets that have reproduction parts. Reproduction parts are poorer in quality than the original. They are usually made of formed copper and have been electroplated. To complete a helmet missing a needed part with a repro item will significantly impact the value of a helmet. It is most onerous when rare front plates are concerned.

2. *We would MUCH rather have an original common helmet than a fake rare one.*

3. Naturally, **rank** has a lot to do with the value of a helmet. Officers' model helmets are more valuable than enlisted models. The purchaser should remember that *officer model helmets must have all the characteristics* required to make the helmet proper for an officer. A helmet that appears to be an officer model but has a spike without officer's 'pearls and diamond' ring, or without "star" retainers, is usually a private purchase helmet of a 1 Year Volunteer or Officer Candidate. Such helmets are not valued as high as that of a full officer model.

4. The collector must remember that most of these helmets are all about 100 years old. **Condition** varies from pristine pieces that have been wonderfully stored in

carrying cases to those found in the attics of Texas farmhouses. In every case, a mint original helmet will bring a premium price on the collector market. Such items are rare to find today. A helmet that is complete but shows slight aging or is dirty will also bring a good price. Helmets that are damaged, altered, or missing parts must be discounted in value relative to the degree of problems.
Most collectors prefer the helmet to remain in its original and unaltered condition. Replacement parts should be utilized only to restore a helmet to its original rank and position. BEWARE of over cleaning. An unskilled restorer can easily ruin a valuable helmet with his zeal to clean up a helmet. As skilled restorers we have harmed pieces by trying too hard. Remember, officer helmets were fire gilded and SHOULD NOT be cleaned with an abrasive metal cleaner.

5. The collector must be aware of the importance of **rarity**. Prussia, being the most heavily populated of the German states, fielded a large contingent in the German army, while the duchy of Schwarzburg Rudolstadt had only one battalion of troops. There were certainly thousands of Prussian helmets to every one helmet from Schwarzburg Rudolstadt. We recommend the collector study the breakdown of the German army regiments to get a clear picture of the relative numbers related to availability of helmet types. The helmets from some regiments bring a premium because of their appearance alone. Besides its rarity, the Braunschweig "Deaths Head" 92nd Infantry Regiment is much sought after due to its haunting beauty. The same is true of Life Guard and elite regiment helmets from all the German states.

The German Pickelhaube had a distinct place in military history. It was the figurehead of one of the greatest national armies the world has ever known. The fantastic shape of the spiked helmet, along with its decoration and shining colors, exemplified the pride of military tradition and the glory of a bygone age. For the collector, each helmet found is a true "***piece of history***."

2

Helmets of the Reserve and Landwehr Troops

The need for manpower in the army of the German States was offset by the high cost of maintaining a large standing army. In order to keep a trained military force ready for a call to the colors, an elaborate system of standing army, active reserve, and militia was designed. To answer the need for trained soldiers, the **Prussian War Ministry** founded the **Reserve Officers Corps** on July 4, 1868. The Reserve Officers were allowed to wear the uniform of an active duty officer, with the exception of the placement of the "***Landwehr Cross***" on the helmet plate. The Reserve and Landwehr contingents were an important part of the German Armie's offensive and defensive strategies. By the beginning of World War I the German Army listed 23,000 Reserve and 11,000 Landwehr Officers.

Beginning in the late 19th century every male German was liable for military service from his 17th to his 45th birthday. At age 17 the youngster was liable to serve in the "**Landsturm 1st Ban**." This category was intended primarily for home defense. When a young man reached his 20th birthday he was liable for service in the regular army. Two years of active service (three years for artillery and cavalry) was followed successively by five years of **Reserve** duty, 11 years in the **Landwehr**, and seven years in the **Landsturm 2nd Ban**.

The German Corp of Officers formed a distinct social and cultural caste. The appointment and promotion remained a royal prerogative, and the holding of a commission carried with it many material and social privileges. A unique pathway to the Officer Ranks was service as a **One Year Volunteer**. Young men from well to do families who undertook to clothe, feed, and equip themselves during their period of service, and who attained a satisfactory standard of efficiency in their duties, were permitted to transfer to the reserve as **Aspirant Officers** at the end of one year's service. After undergoing two annual officer's training sessions with the Reserves and passing the Officer's Examination, the One Year Volunteers were graded as Reserve Officers. By 1913 there were over 15,000 One Year Volunteers in the German Army.

The Prussian War Ministry ordered the use of the "Landwehr Cross" for Reserve Officer and Enlisted Men *A.K.O of February 17, 1869*. For the helmet, the Landwehr/Reserve cross was ordered to be prominently displayed on the middle of the Prussian eagles breast. The *A.K.O. of April 6, 1869* order that eagle front plates that had star devices on their breasts would wear the new Reserve/Landwehr cross under the star. Contingent German States soon adopted their own style of Landwehr Cross for their Reserve units.

The Reserve/Landwehr Army was organized in Military Districts (Landwehr Bezirk). Officers in these districts wore the helmet of the active duty regiment, but with the Landwehr Cross and change in front plate design consistent with their Reserve/Landwehr status. One unique difference was the **Landwehr Officers** of the **92nd Infantry Regiment** (Braunschweig) of the X Army Corps Landwehr District. **Officers of the I and II Battalion wore the Landwehr Cross over the pre-1912 Braunschweig Enameled Star with the Riding Horse without the "Peninsula" banner**, instead of the Skull device used by all the active duty soldiers after 1912.

Prussian Guard Landwehr Officer Model 1897

Prussian Guard Reserve Officer Model 1897

Frontplates of the Reserve and Landwehr

Prussia
Guards
Regiments

Reserve

Landwehr

All Prussian Reserve and Landwehr
Eagles do not wear banner
"Mit Gott fur Koenig...."

Prussia
Grenadier
Regiments

Reserve

Landwehr

Prussia and Oldenburg Reserve Cross

Prussia
Heraldic Eagle
Regt s of the Line

Reserve

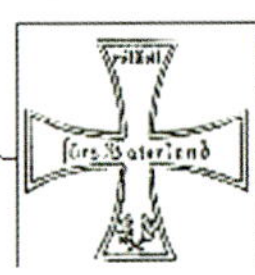

Landwehr

ReserveCross
Hamburg
Luebeck
Bremen

Mecklenburg-Strelitz

Mecklenburg-Schwerin

✠Silver frontplate will carry gold colored reserve cross.✠

Thuringian States and Brunswick

Anhalt
Infantry Regt. 93

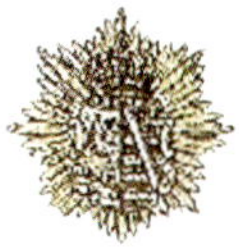

Saxe-Thuringian
Inf. Regt. 95 – 153

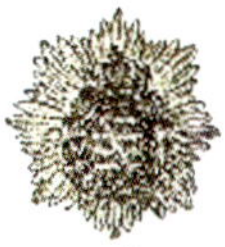

Saxe-Weimar
Inf. Regt. 94

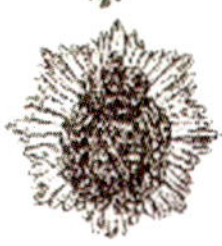

Brunswick
I.R. 92 I-III B
1888-1912

Brunswick
Inf. Regt. 92 II Bat.
1888-1912
After 1912 entire Regt.

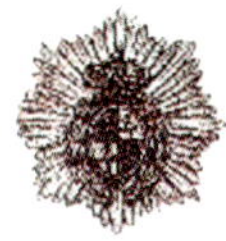

Reuss
Infantry Regt. 96
II Bat.

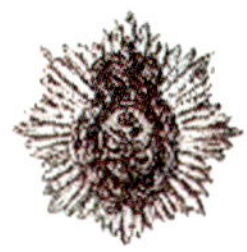

Schwartzburg-Rudolstadt
Inf. Regt. 96
III Bat

Baden LGR109– Reserve and Landwehr

Baden-Reserve and Landwehr

Saxony Reserve– Landw.

Hessen LIR 115– Reserve and Landwehr

Hessen
Reserve
Cross

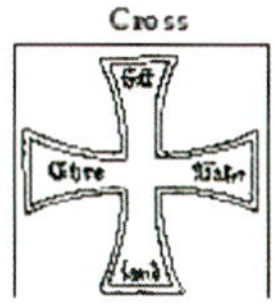

Hessen Reserve and Landwehr

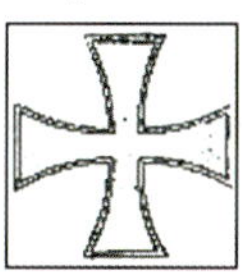

Wurttemberg
Reserve Cross

Wurttemberg Reserve and Landw.

Bavarian
Reserve Cross

Bavaria- Reserve and Landwehr

3

Parade Plumes

A common misconception of collectors today is that all Officers wore plumed helmets when on parade. This is not the case. Of course, Royal Personages and their staffs, General Officers, General Staff, and General Adjutants wore elegant plumes to parade. For the remainder of the Army, plumed helmets were worn only by the officers and other ranks of elite regiments, or by regiments specially honored with the right to wear the plumed helmet.

Although the "Picklehaube" was first used in 1842, the helmet plume was not introduced to service until 1843 (*AKO of April 5*) for use by regiments who were allowed to wear the colored pompom on the older pattern shako. The plume, made of colored straight horse hair, was to be worn in place of the spike for Parade Dress. The plumes were mounted on the helmet by removal of the spike and replacing it with a 13mm plume holder (*trichter*) in the form of an elongated spike. **There were only three colors of plume** (outside of the feathered plumes worn by General Officers) worn by the Imperial German Army. They were **black**, **white**, and **red**. In 1843 the Guard and Guard Grenadier Regiments wore white plumes. The Fusiliers and Regiment No. 8 wore black plumes. For all the units that wore the plume, trumpeters and musicians wore red as a special indication of their service. For Regiments of Foot (i.e. Infantry, Grenadier, etc.), the horse hair plume was cut to the upper seam of the front visor. For Cavalry and Mounted Regiments, the plume was cut to the bottom edge of the visor.

During the evolution of the "Pickelhaube" there were a number of Regiments that were given the honor of wearing plumed helmets. States other than Prussia also adopted the plume for their distinguished Regiments. In 1892 the enlisted pattern trichter changed

Prussian Grenadier Enlisted Mod. 1860 with red plume for trumpeter.

Guard Infantry Enlisted Man with M-1860 Plumed Helmet

from a stylized spike to a tall slender tube-like shape. Horse hair was used by both officers and enlisted men until 1896, when Buffalo hair was allowed to be used for the officer helmet by the General Quartermaster Command.

In 1914 plumed helmets were worn to parade by the following:

GENERAL OFFICERS* and **STAFF:**
PRUSSIA
General Officer, General Adjutant, General a' la Suite
Cock Feathered Plume: **Inside Black - Outside White**

General Staff / War Ministry / Aide de Camp: White Hair Plume

BAVARIA
General Officer, General Adjutant, General a' la Suite
Cock Feathered Plume: **Inside Light Blue - Outside White**

General Staff / War Ministry / Aide de Camp: White Hair Plume

BADEN
Ducal Family Helmet: Feathered Plume: **Inside Red & Yellow - Outside White**
Aide de Camp: White Hair Plume

HESSEN
General Officer, General Adjutant, General a' la Suite
Cock Feathered Plume**: Inside Red - Outside White**

Aide de Camp: White Hair Plume

MECKLENBURG-SCHWERIN
General Officer General Adjutant
Cock Feathered Plume: **Inside Dark Blue - Outside White**

Aide de Camp: White Hair Plume

**Feathered Generals style plumes were often worn by non-General officers who were regimental commanders for parade dress.*
X Regiments that wear plumes will have red plumes for musicians and trumpeter.

Grenadier Officer helmet with Buffalo Plume

Guard Fusiler Regiment Enlisted Helmet to Parade

General Officers Helmets to Parade

SAXONY
General Officer, General Adjutant, General a' la Suite
Vulture Feathered Plume: **All White**

General Staff, War Ministry, Aide de Camp: White Hair Plume

WUERTTEMBERG
General Officer, General Adjutant, General a' la Suite
Cock Feathered Plume: **Inside Black & Red - Outside White**

General Staff, War Ministry, Aide de Camp: White Hair Plume

INFANTRY REGIMENTS:
PRUSSIA
1st Guard Regiment of Foot, I-II Bat. **White**, III Bat. **Black**
2nd Guard Regiment of Foot, I-II Bat. **White**, III Bat. **Black**
1st Guard Grenadier Regt., I-II Bat. **White**, III Bat. **Black**
2nd through 5th Guard Grenadier Regt.s, **White**
Guard Fusilier Regiment, **White**
3rd through 5th Guard Regt.s of Foot, **White**
1st through 12th Grenadier Regt.s, **Black**

25th Infantry Regiment, **Black**
80th Infantry Regiment, **Black**
86th Infantry Regiment, **Black**
145th Kings Infantry Regt., **Black**

MECKLENBURG-SCHWERIN
89th Grenadier Regt., I-III Bat., **Black**

MECKLENBURG-STRELITZ
89th Grenadier Regt., II Bat., **White**

BRAUNSCHWEIG
92nd Infantry Regiment, **Black**

SAXONY
100th Grenadier Regiment, **Black**
101st Grenadier Regiment, **Black**

BADEN
109th Life Guard Gren. Regiment, I-II Bat.**White**, III Bat. **Black**
110th Grenadier Regiment, **White**

HESSEN
115th Life Guard Inf. Regt., **Black**
116th Infantry Regt., Black
117th Life Inf. Regiment, **Black**

WUERTTEMBERG
119th Grenadier Regiment, **White**
120th Infantry Regiment, **Black**
123rd Grenadier Regiment, **Black**

BAVARIA
No Bavarian Infantry Regt.s wore Plumes

PIONEER BATTALIONS:
PRUSSIA
Guard Pioneer Bat., **Black**
3rd Pioneer Bat., **Black**

SAXONY
12th Pioneer Bat., **Black**

Prussian Guard Officer with black buffalo hair parade plume

4

General Officers, General Staff, Adjutants, and Aide de Camp

General von Mackensen in the uniform of a Prussian General.

Preussen/Prussia, also for the state of **Baden**
General Officer, General Adjutant, War Ministry
(Artillery General Officers wear "ball" finial)

Preussen/Prussia, also **Baden**
To Parade
General Officer, General Adjutant, *War Ministry wear white hair plume

Preussen/Prussia
General of Pioneer Corps
General a' la Suite, General Staff

Preussen/Prussia
To Parade
General of Pioneer Corps, General a‘ la Suite, *General Staff wear white hair plume

Baden/Baden
General pattern helmet worn by Baden Royal Family
(to Parade: Yellow/Red/White feather plume)

Baden/Baden
Princely Aide de Camp
(to Parade: White hair bush)

Bayern/Bavaria
General Officer, General a' la Suite
*worn after April 17, 1913

Bayern/Bavaria
To Parade
General Officer, General Staff wear white hair plume, *worn after April 17, 1913

Bayern/Bavaria
General Staff, Aide de Camp to the King
General Officers wore this helmet August 16, 1902-April 17, 1913

Bayern/Bavaria
General Adjutant, Helmet also worn by Artillery General Officer
***worn after April 17, 1913, *after April 6, 1916, Artillery General wore ball finial**

Bayern/Bavaria
War Ministry
Model 1897

Bayern/Bavaria
Colonel serving in Generals Position
Worn 1886 until 1898

Hessen/Hessen
General Officer, 25th Grand Ducal Hessen Division
Worn only by a native citizen Hessen officer, Model 1897

Hessen/Hessen
To Parade, General Officer, 25th Grand Ducal Hessen Division
Worn only by a native Hessen officer, Model 1897

Mecklenburg Schwerin
Mecklenburg Schwerin
General Officer - To Parade
Model 1897

Mecklenburg Schwerin

Mecklenburg Schwerin

Ducal Aide de Camp - To Parade

Model 1897

Sachsen/Saxony
General Officer - General Adjutant - General a'la Suite
Royal Aide de Camp, Model 1897
*Artillery General Officer wore ball finial

Sachsen/Saxony
General Officer - General Adjutant - General a' la Suite
To Parade
Model 1897

Sachsen/Saxony
General Staff Officer
Model 1897

Sachsen/Saxony
General Staff Officer
To Parade
Model 1897

Württemberg/Wurttemberg
General Officer - General Adjutant - War Ministry
Model 1897
*Artillery General wore a ball finial

Württemberg/Wurttemberg
General Officer - General Adjutant
War Ministry wore white hair plume
To Parade, Model 1897

Württemberg/Wurttemberg
General a' la Suite - Aide de Camp to the King
Model 1897
(To Parade: Red/White/Black feathered plume), General Staff (to Parade: White hair plume)

Flags of the Royal House of Germany

Prinz August Wilhelm

5

Imperial German Infantry Regiments

Preussen/Prussia
1st Guard Regiment of Foot
Officer 1st Battalion and Regimental Staff Model 1897

Preussen/Prussia

1st Guard Regimenr of Foot

ENLISTED MAN — 1st Battalion — Model 1871-89

*"Semper Talis" banner added January 27, 1889

Preussen/Prussia
1st Guard Regiment of Foot - 2nd & 3rd Battalion
RESERVE OFFICER
Model 1897

Preussen/Prussia
1st Guard Regimenr of Foot - 2nd & 3rd Battalion
ENLISTED MAN
Model 1895

Preussen/Prussia

2nd, 3rd, & 4th Guard Regiments of Foot

OFFICER — Guard Grenadier Regiments 1, 2, 3, 4, & 5 — Model 1897

Preussen/Prussia
2nd, 3rd, & 4th Guard Regiments of Foot
ENLISTED MAN Guard Grenadier Regiments 1, 2, 3, 4, & 5 Model 1895

Preussen/Prussia

Guard Fusilier Regiment

5th Guard Regiment of Foot

OFFICER — Model 1897

Preussen/Prussia

Guard Fusilier Regiment

ENLISTED MAN 5th Guard Regiment of Foot Model 1895

Prussian Guards enlisted man wearing Parade dress helmet circa 1910.

ENLISTED MAN	**Preussen**/Prussia Guard Regiments	Model 1915

	Preussen/Prussia	
	Grenadier Regiment Crown Prince	
OFFICER	1st East Prussian – Grenadier Regiment No. 1	Model 1897
	(plate worn prior to March 6, 1900)	-until 1890

Preussen/Prussia

Grenadier Regiment Crown Prince

ENLISTED MAN	1st East Prussian – Grenadier Regiment No. 1 Original "**1619**" worn until 1888	Model 1871 -1888

Preussen/Prussia

Grenadier Regiment Crown Prince

OFFICER — 1st East Prussian – Grenadier Regt. No. 1 (Helmet plate worn after March 6, 1900) — Model 1897-after 1900

Preussen/Prussia

Grenadier Regiment Crown Prince

ENLISTED MAN — 1st East Prussian – Grenadier Regt. No. 1 (Helmet plate worn after March 6, 1900) — Model 1895-after 1900

	Preussen/Prussia	
OFFICER	Grenadier Regiments 5, 6, 10, 11, & 12 Helmet plate used before 1912	Model 1897 until 1912

Preussen/Prussia

ENLISTED MAN — Grenadier Regiments 5, 6, 10, 11, & 12 — Model 1895

Helmet plate used before 1912 — until 1912

Preussen/Prussia

OFFICER Grenadiers Regiments 2, 3, & 8 (**Prior to 1912**) Model 1897
Grenadier Regiments 5, 6, 10, 11, & 12 (**After 1912**)

Preussen/Prussia

ENLISTED MAN — Grenadiers Regiments 2, 3, & 8 (**Prior to 1912**) — Model 1895

Grenadier Regimens 5, 6, 10, 11, & 12 (**After 1912**)

Preussen/Prussia

OFFICER	Grenadier Regiment King Frederick the Great 3rd East Prussian, Regiment No. 4 Helmet plate used before 1911	Model 1897 until 1911

Preussen/Prussia

OFFICER	Grenadier Regiment King Frederick the Great	Model 1897
	3rd East Prussian, Regiment No. 4	after 1911
	Helmet plate used after 1911	

	Preussen/Prussia	
ENLISTED MAN	Grenadier Regiment King Frederick the Great 3rd East Prussian, Regiment No. 4 Helmet plate used after 1911	Model 1895 after 1911

Preussen/Prussia

OFFICER — Grenadier Regiment King Wilhelm I — Model 1897

2nd East Prussian, Regiment No. 7

Banner "**22 Marz 1797**" awarded March 22, 1897

Prince Oscar of Prussia in the helmet and uniform of the 7th Grenadier Regiment.

Preussen/Prussia

OFFICER Grenadier Regiment King Frederick Wilhelm III Model 1897

1st Brandenburg, Regiment No. 8

Officer Rosette:

7th Grenadier Regiment

Officer Rosette:

8th Grenadier Regiment

8th Grenadier Enlisted M91 side lugs

1st & 3rd Bat. 2nd Bat.

Preussen/Prussia

OFFICER	Colberg Grenadier Regiment Graf Gniesenau 2nd Pommeranian, Regiment No. 9 Helmet plate used before June 16, 1913	Model 1897 until 1913

Preussen/Prussia

NCO	Colberg Grenadier Regiment Graf Gniesenau	Model 1897
	2nd Pommeranian, Regiment No. 9	until 1913
	Helmet plate used before June 16, 1913	

Preussen/Prussia

OFFICER	Colberg Grenadier Regiment Graf Gniesenau 2nd Pommeranian, Regiment No. 9 Helmet plate used after June 16, 1913	Model 1897 after 1913

Preussen/Prussia

ENLISTED	Colberg Grenadier Regiment Graf Gniesenau	Model 1895
MAN	2nd Pommeranian, Regiment No. 9	until 1913
	Helmet plate used before June 16, 1913	

Preussen/Prussia

OFFICER — Kings Infantry Regiment No. 145 — Model 1897

6th Lorraine Infantry Regiment

Preussen/Prussia

ENLISTED MAN — Kings Infantry Regiment No. 145 — Model 1895

6th Lorraine Infantry Regiment

Preussen/Prussia

OFFICER — Infantry Regiments of the Line — Model 1897

No.s 13-33, 35-72, 75, 76, 79-86, 96-1st Bat., 97-99, 128-133, 135-138, 140, 141, 143, 144, 146-152, 154-163, 166, 167, 171-176

Preussen/Prussia

OFFICER Line Infantry Regiments to Parade Model 1897

No.s 25, 80, 86

Preussen/Prussia

ENLISTED MAN Infantry Regiments of the Line Model 1895

No.s 13-33, 35-72, 75, 76, 79-86, 96-1st Bat., 97-99, 128-133, 135-138, 140, 141, 143, 144, 146-152, 154-163, 166, 167, 171-176

Preussen/Prussia

ENLISTED MAN Infantry Regiments of the Line Model 1915

No.s 13-33, 35-72, 75, 76, 79-86, 96-1st Bat., 97-99, 128-133, 135-138, 140, 141, 143, 144, 146-152, 154-163, 166, 167, 171-176

Preussen/Prussia

OFFICER Fusilier Regiment Queen Victoria of Sweden No. 34 Model 1897

Fusilier Regiment Cont Roon No. 33, 5-6 Companies

Preussen/Prussia

ENLISTED MAN — Fusilier Regiment Queen Victoria of Sweden No. 34 — Model 1895

Fusilier Regiment Cont Roon No. 33, 5-6 Companies

Hannover/Hannover

OFFICER — Fusilier Regiment General Field Marshall Prince Albrecht of Prussia No. 73 — Model 1897 after 1899

Banner "**Peninsula-Waterloo**" awarded January 24, 1899

Hannover/Hannover

ENLISTED MAN Fusilier Regiment General Field Marshall Prince Albrecht of Prussia No. 73 — Model 1895 after 1899

Banner "**Peninsula-Waterloo**" awarded January 24, 1899

Hannover/Hannover

Hannoverian Infantry Regiments No.s 74, 77, 78, 164, & 165

OFFICER — Banner "**Waterloo**" awarded January 24, 1899 — Model 1897 after 1899

Hannover/Hannover

Hannoverian Infantry Regiments No.s 74, 77, 78, 164, & 165

ENLISTED MAN	Banner "**Waterloo**" awarded January 24, 1899	Model 1895 after 1899

ENLISTED MAN	**Hannover**/Hannover Fusilier Regiment General Field Marshall Prince Albrecht of Prussia No. 73	Model 1915

Hannover/Hannover

Hannoverian Infantry Regiments No.s 74, 77, 78, 164, & 165

ENLISTED MAN Model 1915

Nassau/Nassau

OFFICER — 1st Nassau Infantry Regiment No. 87 — Model 1897

Banner "**LaBelle-Alliance**" awarded January 24, 1899 — after 1899

Nassau/Nassau

ENLISTED MAN 1st Nassau Infantry Regiment No. 87 Model 1895

Banner "**LaBelle-Alliance**" awarded January 24, 1899 after 1899

Nassau/Nassau

OFFICER	2nd Nassau Infantry Regiment No. 88	Model 1897
	Banner "**LaBelle-Alliance-Mesa de Ibor-Medellin**"	after 1899
	awarded January 24, 1899	

Nassau/Nassau

ENLISTED	2nd Nassau Infantry Regiment No. 88	Model 1895
MAN	Banner "**LaBelle-Alliance-Mesa de Ibor-Medellin**"	after 1899
	awarded January 24, 1899	

Mecklenburg-Strelitz/Mecklenburg-Strelitz

OFFICER | Grand Ducal Grenadier Regiment No. 89 – 2nd Battalion | Model 1897

Mecklenburg-Strelitz/Mecklenburg-Strelitz

ONE YEAR VOLUNTEER	Grand Ducal Grenadier Regiment No. 89 – 2nd Battalion	Model 1897

Mecklenburg Schwerin/Mecklenburg-Schwerin

OFFICER — Grand Ducal Grenadier Regiment No. 89 – 1st & 3rd Battalion — Model 1897

Grand Ducal Fusilier Regiment No. 90

Mecklenburg Schwerin/Mecklenburg-Schwerin

RESERVE OFFICER

Grand Ducal Grenadier Regiment No. 89 – 1st & 3rd Battalion
Grand Ducal Fusilier Regiment No. 90

Model 1897

Young soldier from the 90th Fusilier Regiment circa 1914.

Mecklenburg Schwerin/Mecklenburg-Schwerin

ENLISTED MAN

Grand Ducal Grenadier Regiment No. 89 – 1st & 3rd Battalion
Grand Ducal Fusilier Regiment No. 90

Model 1895

Mecklenburg-Strelitz/Mecklenburg Strelitz		
ENLISTED MAN	Grand Ducal Grenadier Regiment No. 89 – 2nd Battalion	Model 1915

Mecklenburg Schwerin/Mecklenburg-Schwerin

ENLISTED MAN — Grand Ducal Grenadier Regiment No. 89 – 1st & 3rd Battalion; Grand Ducal Fusilier Regiment No. 90 — Model 1915

Oldenburg/Oldenburg

OFFICER — Oldenburg Infantry Regiment No. 91 — Model 1897

ONE YEAR VOLUNTEER	**Oldenburg**/Oldenburg Oldenburg Infantry Regiment No. 91	Model 1897

Oldenburg/Oldenburg

ENLISTED MAN Oldenburg Infantry Regiment No. 91 Model 1895

Oldenburg/Oldenburg

ENLISTED MAN Oldenburg Infantry Regiment No. 91 Model 1915

Braunschweig/Brunswick

OFFICER — Brunswick Infantry Regiment — Model 1897

No. 92 – 2nd Battalion (before 1912)

Helmet plate used by entire Regiment after 1912

Braunschweig/Brunswick

OFFICER — Brunswick Infantry Regiment — Model 1897

No. 92 – 2nd Battalion (before 1912)

Helmet plate used by entire Regiment after 1912

Braunschweig/Brunswick

ENLISTED MAN — Brunswick Infantry Regiment — Model 1889

No. 92 – 2nd Battalion (before 1912)

Helmet plate used by entire Regiment after 1912,

(first issue spiked helmet for Brunswick)

Braunschweig/Brunswick

ENLISTED MAN Brunswick Infantry Regiment No. 92 Model 1915

Braunschweig/Brunswick

OFFICER — Brunswick Infantry Regiment — Model 1897

No. 92 – 1st & 3rd Battalions (before 1912)

Helmet plate replaced by "Skull" after 1912 for active duty soldiers

Brunswick 92nd Infantry Reserve Officer circa 1900.

Braunschweig/Brunswick

LANDWEHR OFFICER — Brunswick Infantry Regiment No. 92 – 1st & 3rd Battalions (before 1912) — Model 1897

Helmet plate worn by Officers of the 10th Army Corp Reserve District after 1912. *Note absence of "**Peninsula**" banner under star.

Braunschweig/Brunswick

RESERVE OFFICER Brunswick Infantry Regiment Model 1897

No. 92 – 1st & 3rd Battalions (before 1912)

Helmet plate used only by Reserve Officers after 1912

Anhalt/Anhalt

OFFICER	Anhalt Infantry Regiment No. 93	Model 1897

Anhalt/Anhalt

ENLISTED MAN Anhalt Infantry Regiment No. 93 Model 1895

	Sachsen-Weimar/Saxe-Wemar	
OFFICER	Infantry Regiment Grand Duke of Saxony 5th Thuringian, Regiment No. 94	Model 1897

Sachsen-Weimar/Saxe-Wemar

ENLISTED MAN — Infantry Regiment Grand Duke of Saxony 5th Thuringian, Regiment No. 94 — Model 1895

Sachsen-Thüringen/Saxe-Thuringia

OFFICER — 6th Thuringian Infantry Regiment No. 95 — Model 1897

8th Thuringian Infantry Regiment No. 153

	Sachsen-Thüringen/Saxe-Thuringia	
RESERVE OFFICER	6th Thuringian Infantry Regiment No. 95 8th Thuringian Infantry Regiment No. 153	Model 1897

Reuss/Reuss

OFFICER	7th Thuringian Infantry Regiment No. 96 - 2nd Battalion	Model 1897

ENLISTED MAN	**Reuss**/Reuss 7th Thuringian Infantry Regiment No. 96 - 2nd Battalion	Model 1895

Schwarzburg-Rudolstadt/Schwartzburg-Rudolstadt

OFFICER — 7th Thuringian Infantry Regiment No. 96 – 3rd Battalion — Model 1897

Schwarzburg-Rudolstadt/Schwartzburg-Rudolstadt

ENLISTED MAN — 7th Thuringian Infantry Regiment No. 96 – 3rd Battalion — Model 1895

	Sachsen/Saxony	
OFFICER	Royal Saxon 1st (Life Guard) Grenadier Regiment No. 100	Model 1897

ENLISTED MAN	Sachsen/Saxony Royal Saxon 1st (Life Guard) Grenadier Regiment No. 100	Model 1895

Sachsen/Saxony

OFFICER — Royal Saxon Rifle (Fusilier) Regiment Prince Johann George No. 108 — Circa 1910

ENLISTED MAN	**Sachsen**/Saxony Royal Saxon Rifle (Fusilier) Regiment Prince Johann George No. 108	Circa 1900

Sachsen/Saxony

OFFICER Royal Saxon Grenadier Regiment 101 Model 1897

Infantry Regiments 102-107, 133, 134, 139, 177-179 & 181

Young Saxon Soldier circa 1910

Sachsen/Saxony

ENLISTED	Royal Saxon Grenadier Regiment 101	Model 1895
MAN	Infantry Regiments 102-107, 133, 134, 139, 177-179 & 181	

Sachsen/Saxony

ENLISTED MAN — Royal Saxon Grenadier Regiment 101 — Model 1915

Infantry Regiments 102-107, 133, 134, 139, 177-179 & 181

Baden/Baden

OFFICER 1st Baden Life Guard Grenadier Regiment No. 109 Model 1897

Baden/Baden

RESERVE OFFICER

1st Baden Life Guard Grenadier Regiment No. 109 – 1st & 2nd Battalion to Parade (3rd Battalion wore black hair plume)

Model 1897

Baden/Baden

RESERVE OFFICER | 1st Baden Life Guard Grenadier Regiment No. 109 | Model 1897

Baden/Baden		
ENLISTED MAN	1st Baden Life Guard Grenadier Regiment No. 109	Model 1895

Baden/Baden

OFFICER — Grenadier Regiment No. 110 — Model 1897

Infantry Regiments 111-114, 142, 169 & 170

Baden/Baden

RESERVE	Grenadier Regiment No. 110	Model 1895
ENLISTED	Infantry Regiments 111-114, 142, 169 & 170	
MAN		

Baden Infantryman circa 1914.

Baden/Baden

ENLISTED MAN — Grenadier Regiment No. 110 — Model 1915

Infantry Regiments 111-114, 142, 169 & 170

	Hessen/Hessen	
RESERVE	Life Guard Infantry Regiment No. 115	Model 1871
OFFICER	Grand Ducal Hessen Infantry Regiment	used until 1897

Hessen/Hessen

ENLISTED MAN	Life Guard Infantry Regiment No. 115 Grand Ducal Hessen Infantry Regiment	Model 1895 used until 1897

Hessen/Hessen

OFFICER — Life Guard Infantry Regiment No. 115 — Model 1897

Grand Ducal Hessen Infantry Regiment

	Hessen/Hessen	
ENLISTED MAN	Life Guard Infantry Regiment No. 115 Grand Ducal Hessen Infantry Regiment	Model 1895

Hessen/Hessen

OFFICER — Infantry Regiments No. 116, 118 & 168 — Model 1897

Hessen/Hessen

ENLISTED MAN	Infantry Regiments No. 116, 118 & 168	Model 1895

Hessen/Hessen

OFFICER Infantry Life Guard Regiment Grand Duchess No. 117 Model 1897
Banner "**1697-1897**" awarded in 1897

Hessen/Hessen

ENLISTED MAN	Infantry Life Guard Regiment Grand Duchess No. 117 Banner "**1697-1897**" awarded in 1897	Model 1895

Hessen/Hessen

OFFICER — Infantry Life Guard Regiment — Model 1897-1915

Grand Duchess No. 117 -9th Company

Banner "**1697-1897**" awarded in 1897

ENLISTED MAN	Hessen/Hessen Infantry Life Guard Regiment Grand Duchess No. 117 -9th Company Banner "**1697-1897**" awarded in 1897	Model 1895

Hessen/Hessen

ENLISTED MAN | All Infantry Regiments | Model 1915 (first pattern)

ENLISTED MAN	**Hessen**/Hessen All Infantry Regiments	Model 1915 (later pattern)

Württemberg/Wurttemberg

OFFICER — Grenadier Regiments Queen Olga (1st Wurttemberg) No. 119 — Model 1897

Grenadier Regiment King Karl (5th Wurttemberg) No. 123

Württemberg/Wurttemberg

ENLISTED MAN — Grenadier Regiments Queen Olga (1st Wurttemberg) No. 119 — Model 1895

Grenadier Regiment King Karl (5th Wurttemberg) No. 123

Württemberg/Wurttemberg

OFFICER Infantry Regiments No. 120-122, 124-127, & 180 Model 1897

OFFICER	**Württemberg**/Wurttemberg Infantry Regiments No. 120-122, 124-127, & 180	Model 1897-1915

Württemberg/Wurttemberg

ENLISTED MAN	Infantry Regiments No. 120-122, 124-127, & 180	Model 1895

Württemberg/Wurttemberg		
ENLISTED MAN	All Infantry, Grenadier and Pioneer Troops	Model 1915

	Bayern/Bavaria	
OFFICER	Infantry Life Guard Regiment	Model 1897

Bayern/Bavaria

ENLISTED MAN — Infantry Life Guard Regiment — Model 1896

Bayern/Bavaria

OFFICER | Infantry Regiments No. 1-23 | Model 1897

Bayern/Bavaria

ENLISTED MAN | Infantry Regiments No. 1-23 | Model 1896

Bayern/Bavaria

ENLISTED MAN	All Infantry Regiments and Pioneer Battalions	Model 1915

6

Imperial German Pioneer (Engineer) Battalions

Pioneer Battalions of the Imperial German Army.

	Preussen/Prussia	
OFFICER	Guard Pioneer Battalion	Model 1897

Preussen/Prussia

ENLISTED MAN | Guard Pioneer Battalion | Model 1895

Preussen/Prussia

OFFICER — Pioneer Battalion Count Radziwill No. 1 — Model 1897

Pioneer Battalion von Rauch No. 3

Preussen/Prussia		
ENLISTED MAN	Pioneer Battalion Count Radziwill No. 1 Pioneer Battalion von Rauch No. 3	Model 1895

Preussen/Prussia

OFFICER Pioneer Battalions No. 2, 4-9, 11, 15-21, & 23-30 Model 1897

Preussen/Prussia

ENLISTED MAN	Pioneer Battalions No. 2, 4-9, 11, 15-21, & 23-30	Model 1895

Hannover/Hannover

OFFICER — Pioneer Battalion No. 10 — Model 1897

Hannover/Hannover

ENLISTED MAN — Pioneer Battalion No. 10 — Model 1895

	Sachsen/Saxony	
OFFICER	Pioneer Battalions No. 12 & 22	Model 1897

Sachsen/Saxony		
ENLISTED MAN	Pioneer Battalions No. 12 & 22	Model 1895

Württemberg/Wurttemberg

OFFICER	Pioneer Battalion No. 13	Model 1897

	Württemberg/Wurttemberg	
ENLISTED MAN	Pioneer Battalion No. 13	Model 1895

Baden/Baden

OFFICER	Pioneer Battalion No. 14	Model 1897

Baden/Baden

ENLISTED MAN | Pioneer Battalion No. 14 | Model 1895

Bayern/Bavaria

OFFICER	Pioneer Battalions No. 1-4	Model 1897

Bayern/Bavaria

ENLISTED MAN | Pioneer Battalions No. 1-4 | Model 1896

Appendix A:

Quartermasters Regulation for Officers and Medical Officers of the Royal Prussian Army Berlin-1911

Bekleidungs-Vorschrift fur Offiziere und Sanitats Offiziere des Koenigliche Preussischen Heeres Berlin-1911

The following is a translation of the Royal Prussian Quartermaster Regulations for the fabrication of Officer helmets as printed by Mittler & Sohn in 1911.

Chapter 93

The helmet is to be made of black lacquered leather. When worn, the helmet must rest over the middle of the face with the bottom edge of the front visor equal to the level of the eyebrows and about 3cm over the ears.

Helmet design and measurement:

a. The height of the helmet body must be between 10.5 and 12.5 cm.
b. Front visor width;
a. Rounded visor - 4cm
b. Squared Visor – 3.8cm
c. Metal Visor Tim - .6cm
c. Back Visor width 4.3cm.
d. Back Spine width 1.4cm and is made without a ventilation sleeve. For Dragoon helmet the back spine is not fixed with a domed stud like is used by the enlisted pattern helmet.

Anzugsarten preußischer Infanterie um 1912

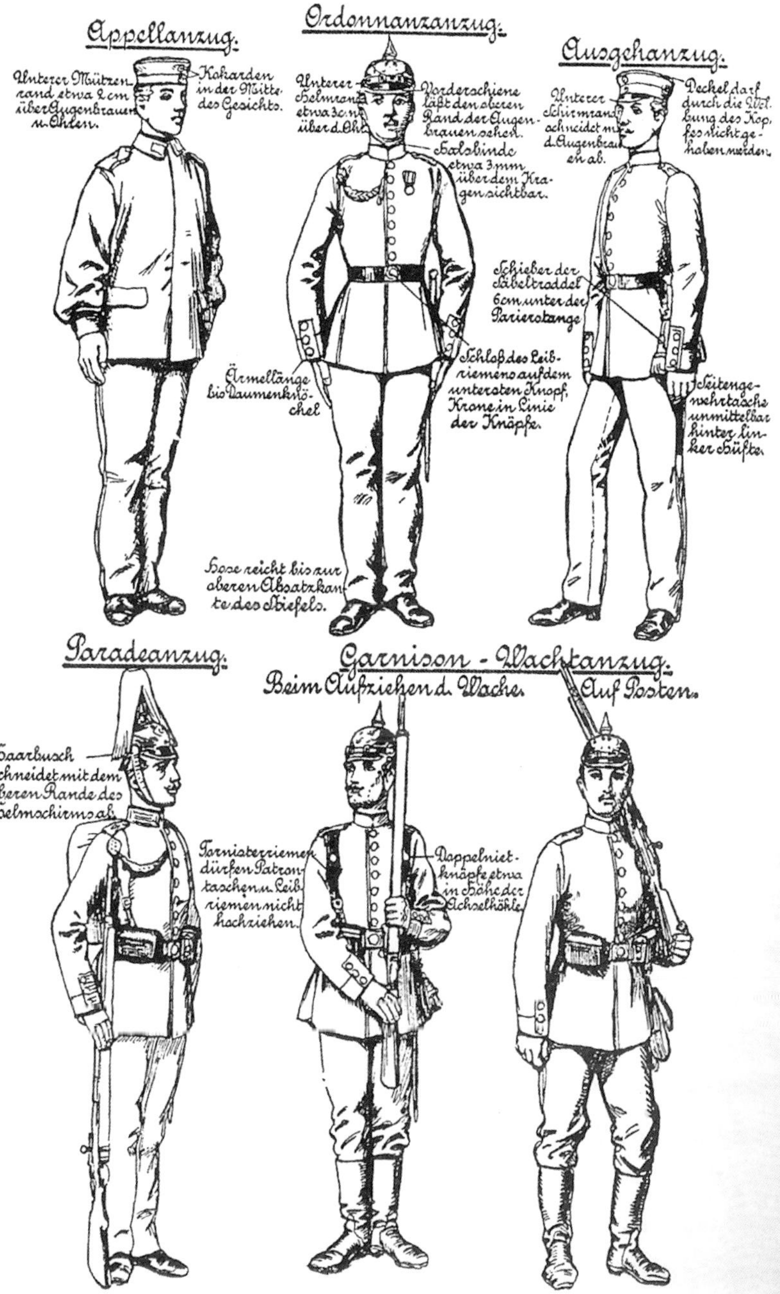

e. Rounded spike base diameter is 8cm. The crossed spike base has a ridged edge with 4wings. Three wings are 7 cm long with the front wing 4cm long. The spike throat will have two ventilation les and have a height of 2.5 cm. The throat is ornamented at its base with the officer style pearl ring. Height of the spike is 7cm or 4.5 for the artillery ball. The spike is smooth except for the 1st Guard of Foot whose officers wear a six sided fluted spike like those worn by General Officers.

f. Spike base is secured to the helmet with four eight pointed gold stars except for the 1st Guard Regiment of Foot which wears silver stars.

g. Chinscales for the for troops of foot will have the flat form and measure 1.3 cm wide at the front and 2.3 cm wide at the back with a 2.5 cm rosette. Chinscales for the mounted troops will have the rounded form and measure 1.4 cm at the front and 2.6 cm wide at the back with a 2.7 X 3.2 cm elongated rosette.

   Chinscales are gold except for the 1st Guard Regiment of Foot who will wear silver. Chinscales will be linked on the right with a metal knob and on the left with an elongated hole. When closed the chinscales must rest firmly on the top edge of the front visor. Chinscales worn under the chin must rest flat against the cheek with the buckle on the left side under the jaw. The chinscale rosette is the color of the uniform button. Grenadier Regiments 7 and 8 will wear the Royal Monogram as found on the epaulettes on the rosette.

h. Cockade diameter is 5.5cm. On the left side is he state cockade. The national (Reichs) cockade is worn on the right side. The middle field of the cockade must be visible behind the chinscale rosette.

i. The front plate must rest directly above the sewn front visor. The heraldic eagle measures 11cm with crown (Crown measures 1.5 cm) and 14 cm wide. The Guard eagle measures 12.7 with crown (Crown measures 1.7 cm) and 28 cm wide. The Silver Guard Star is 9 cm wide and has at its center an enameled Black Eagle on a circular background. The script will be in gold. The golden wreath is ornamented in green and brown enamel.

j. For units such as the I and II Battalion of the 34th Fusilier Regiment that carry the award banner (Queen of Sweden bodyguard unit), all Officers may wear the award. For units of Company or Battery size, only Officers attached to the unit may wear the award banner.

k. The plume will be made of white or black buffalo hair. The trichter in the form of an elongated spike, measures 15 cm and is smooth except for the 1st Guard Regiment of Foot, and has a 4.5 cm diameter removable button on top. For troops of foot the bush is cut to the top edge of the front visor. Mounted troops wear plumes to the bottom edge of the front visor.

Enlisted and non-commissioned officers were issued uniforms, helmets and equipment by the army (Kammerstuecken). One year Volunteers and Officers were required to purchase their own equipment. For a 2nd Lieutenant earning 102 Reich Marks (RM) per month, the purchase of a 26 RM helmet with a 22 RM parade plume along with a Visor Hat 6 RM, Tunic for 37 RM, Pants for 12 RM and a sword for 27 RM one can see that the uniform represented a significant investment of the part of the officer.

Appendix B:
Infantry Regiments of 1914

Frontplate numbers on pages 30-31

Regiment	Est.	Hdq.	Frontplate
1st Guard of Foot	1688	Potsdam	2 -3
2nd Guard of Foot	1813	Berlin	1
1st Guard Gren. Regt. Kaiser Alexander	1814	Berlin	1
2nd Guard. Gren Regt. Kaiser Franz	1814	Berlin	1
Guard Fusilier Regt.	1826	Berlin	3
3rd Guard of Foot	1860	Berlin	1
4th Guard of Foot	1860	Berlin	1
3rd Guard Gren. Regt. Queen Elisabeth	1860	Charlottenburg	1
4th Guard Gren. Regt. Queen Augusta	1860	Berlin	1
5th Guard of Foot	1897	Spandau	3
1st Grenadier Regt. Crown Prince	1655	Koenigsberg/Pr	4a-4b
2nd Grenadier Regt. King Friedrich	1679	Stettin	8a
3rd Grenadier Regt. King Friedrich Wilhelm 1	1685	Koenigsberg/Pr	8a
4th Grenadier Regt. King Friedrich the Great	1626	Rastenburg	5a-5b

5th Grenadier Regt. King Friedrich I	1689	Danzig	8a-8b
6th Grenadier Regt. Graf Kleist von Nollendorf	1772	Posen	8a-8b
7th Grenadier Rgt. King Wilhelm I	1797	Liegnitz	6
8th Life Grenadier Regt. King Friedrich Wilhelm III	1808	Frankfurt/oder	8a
Colberg 9th Gren. Regt. Graf Gneisenau	1808	Stargardi/ Pomm.	7a-7b
10th Grenadier Rgt. King Friedrich Wilhelm II	1808	Schweidnitz	8a-8b
11th Grenadier Regt. King Friedrich III	1808	Breslau	8a-8b
12th Grenadier Regt. Prince Carl of Prussia	1813	Frankfurt/o	8a-8b
13th Infantry Regt. Herwarth von Bittenfeld	1813	Munster	9
14th Infantry Regt. Graf Schwerin	1813	Bromberg	9
15th Infantry Regt. Friederich der Niederlande	1813	Minden	9
16th Infantry Regt. Freiherr von Sparr	1813	Cologne	9
17th Infantry Regt. Graf Barfuss	1813	Morchingen	9
18th Infantry Regt. von Grolman	1813	Osterode	9
19th Infantry Regt. von Courbiere Lauban	1813	Gorlitz	9
20th Infantry Regt. Graf Tauentzien von Wittb.	1813	Wittenberg	9
21st Infantry Regt.	1813	Thorn von Borcke	9
22nd Infantry Regt. Keith Kattowitz	1813	Gleiwitz	9
23rd Infantry Regt. von Winterfeldt	1813	Neisse	9
24th Infantry Regt.	1813	Neuruppin	9

Friedrich Franz II von Meckl. Schw.			
25th Infantry Regt.	1813	Aachen	9
von Lutzow			
26th Infantry Regt.	1813	Magdeburg	9
Leopold v. Anhalt-Dessau			
27th Infantry Regt	1815	Halberstadt	9
Louis Friederich v. Prussia			
28th Infantry Regt.	1813	Ehrenbreitstein / Koblenz	9
von Goeben			
29th Infantry Regt.	1813	Trier	9
von Horn			
30th Infantry Regt.	1812	Saarlouis	9
Graf Werder			
31st Infantry Regt.	1812	Altona	9
Graf Bose			
32nd Infantry Regt.	1815	Meiningen	9
33rd Fusilier Regt.	1749	Gumbinnen	9-10
Graf Roon			
34th Fusilier Regt.	1720	Stettin	10
Queen Viktoria of Sweden		Swinemde	
35th Fusilier Regt.	1815	Brandenburg	9
Prince Heinrich von Prussia	a. H.		
36th Fusilier Regt.	1815	Halle a. S.	9
Feldm. Graf v. Blumenthal	Bernburg		
37th Fusilier Regt.	1818	Krotochin	9
von Steinmetz			
38th Fusilier Regt.	1818	Glatz	9
Feldm. Graf von Molke			
39th Fusilier Regt.	1818	Dusseldorf	9
General Ludendorff			
40th Fusilier Regt.	1818	Rastatt	9
Karl Anton v. Hohenzollern			
41st Infantry Regt.	1860	Tilsit	9
von Boyen	Memel		
42nd Infantry Regt.	1860	Stralsund	9
Moritz v. Anhalt-Dessau	Griefswald		

43rd Infantry Regt.	1860	Koenigsberg/Pillau	9
Duke Karl v. Meckl. Strelitz			
44th Infantry Regt	1860	Goldap	9
Graf Donhoff			
45th Infantry Regt	1860	Insterburg	9
Darkehmen			
46th Infantry Regt.	1860	Posen	9
Graf Kirchberg Wreschen			
47th Infantry Regt.	1860	Posen	9
King Ludwig III of Bavaria	Schrimm		
48th Infantry Regt.	1860	Kustrin	9
von Stuelpnagel			
49th Infantry Regt.	1860	Gnesen	9
50th Infantry Regt.	1860	Rawitsch	9
Lissa			
51st Infantry Regt.	1860	Breslau	9
52nd Infantry Regt.	1860	Cottbus	9
von Alvensleben Krossen			
53rd Infantry Regt.	1860	Cologne	9
54th Infantry Regt.	1860	Kolberg	9
von der Goltz Koslin			
55th Infantry Regt.	1860	Detmold, Horter	9
Graf Bulow v. Dennewitz		Bielefeld	
56th Infantry Regt.	1860	Wesel	9
Vogel von Falkenstein Cleve			
57th Infantry Regt.	1860	Wesel	9
Duke Ferdinand v. Braunschw.			
58th Infantry Regt.	1860	Golgau Fraustadt	9
59th Infantry Regt.	1860	Otsch, Eylau Goldau	9
Freiherr Hiller v. Gaertringen			
60th Infantry Regt.	1860	Weissenberg	9
Markgraf Karl			
61st Infantry Regt.	1860	Thorn	9
von der Marwitz			
62nd Infantry Regt.	1860	Cosel Ratibor	9

63rd Infantry Regt.	1860	Oppeln Lublinitz	9
Kaiser Karl v. Austria & King of Hungary			
64th Infantry Regt.	1860	Prenzlau	9
Gen Feldm. Freiherr Karl v. Pr. Angermunde			
65th Infantry Regt.	1860	Cologne	9
66th Infantry Regt.	1860	Magdeburg	9
67th Infantry Regt.	1860	Metz	9
68th Infantry Regt.	1860	Koblenz	9
69th Infantry Regt.	1860	Trier	9
70th Infantry Regt.	1860	Saarbrucken	9
71st Infantry Regt.	1860	Erfurt Sondershausen	9
72nd Infantry Regt.	1860	Torgau Eilenburg	9
73rd Fusiler Regt.	1803	Hannover	11
Prince Albrecht v. Prussia			
74th Infantry Regt.	1813	Hannover	12
75th Infantry Regt.	1866	Bremen Stade	9
76th Infantry Regt.	1866	Hamburg	9
77th Infantry Regt.	1813	Celle	12
78th Infantry Regt.	1813	Osnabruck Aurich	12
Duke Friedrich Wilh. v. Braunsch.			
79th Infantry Regt.	1813	Hildesheim	9
von Voigts Rhetz			
80th Infantry Regt.	1813	Wiesbaden	9
von Gersdorff		Homb u. d. H	
81st Infantry Regt.	1813	Franfurt a. M	9
Landgraf Friedrich I v. Hesse Kassel			
82nd Infantry Regt.	1813	Gottingen	9
83rd Infantry Regt.	1813	Kassel Arolsen	9
von Wittich			
84th Infantry Regt.	1866	Schleswig Hadersleben	9
von Mannstein			
85th Infantry Regt.	1866	Rendelsberg	9
Duke of Holstein	Kiel		
86th Fusilier Regt.	1866	Flensburg Sonderburg	9
Queen's Regt.			
87th Infantry Regt.	1809	Mainz	13
1st Nassau			

88th Infantry Regt. 2nd Nassau	1808	Mainz Hanau	14
89th Grenadier Regt. Grand Duke of Mecklenburg	1782	Schwerin Neustrelitz	15-16
90th Fusiler Regt. Kaiser Wilhelm	1788	Rostock Wismar	16
91st Infantry Regt. Oldenburg Infantry Regt.	1813	Oldenburg	17
92nd Infantry Regt. Braunschweig Inf. Regt	1809	Braunschweig	18-19
93rd Infantry Regt. Anhalt Infantry Regt	1807	Zerbst Dessau	20
94th Infantry Regt. Grand Duke of Saxony	1702	Weimar Eisenach, Jena	22
95th Infantry Regt.	1807	Gotha, Hildburghausen, Koburg	21
96th Infantry Regt.	1867	Gera Rudolstadt	9-23-24
97th Infantry Regt.	1881	Saarburg	9
98th Infantry Regt.	1881	Metz	9
99th Infantry Regt.	1881	Zabern Pfalzburg	9
100th Life. Gren. Regt. Royal Saxon Life Guard Regt.	1670	Dresden	25
101st Grenadier Regt. Kaiser Wilhelm, King of Prussia	1670	Dresden	26
102nd Infantry Regt. King Ludwig III of Bavaria	1709	Zittau	26
103rd Infantry Regt.	1709	Bautzen	26
104th Infantry Regt.	1701	Chemnitz	26
105th Infantry Regt. King Wilhelm II of Wurttemberg	1701	Strassburg I E.	26
106th Infantry Regt. King Georg	1708	Leipzig	26
107th Infantry Ergt. Prince Johann Georg	1708	Leipzig	26
108th Fusiler/Schutzen R. Prince Georg	1809	Dresden	
109th Life Gren. Regt. Baden Life Guard Regt.	1803	Karlsruhe	27

110th Grenadier Regt.	1852	Mannheim Heidelberg	28
Kaiser Wilhelm I			
111th Infantry Regt.	1852	Rastatt	28
Markgraf Ludwig Wilhelm			
112th Infantry Regt.	1852	Mulhausen i. E	28
Prince Wilhelm			
113th Infantry Regt.	1861	Freiburg i. B	28
114th Infantry Regt.	1867	Konstanz	28
		Burg. Hohenzollern	
115th Life Guard Inf. Regt.	1621	Darmstadt	29a-29b
Grand Duke of Hessen Life Guard Regt.			
116th Infantry Regt.	1813	Giessen	30
117th Life Regt. Duchess	1697	Mainz	31-32
118th Infantry Regt.	1791	Worms	30
119th Grenadier Regt.	1673	Stuttgart	33
Queen Olga			
120th Infantry Regt.	1673	Ulm	34
Kaiser Wilhelm, King of Prussia			
121st Infantry Regt.	1716	Ludwigsburg	34
Old Wurttemberg Regiment			
122nd Infantry Regt.	1806	Heilbronn	34
Kaiser Franz Joseph of Austria		Mergenthal	
123rd Grenadier Regt.	1799	Ulm	33
King Karl			
124th Infantry Regt.	1673	Weingarten	34
King Wilhelm I			
125th Infantry Regt.	1809	Stuttgart	34
Kaiser Friedrich, King of Prussia			
126th Infantry Regt.	1716	Straussburg i. E	34
Grand Duke Friedrich of Baden			
127th Infantry Regt.	1897	Ulm Wiblingen	34
128th Infantry Regt.	1881	Danzig Neufahrwasser	9
129th Infantry Regt.	1881	Graudenz	9
Gen. Feldm. V. Mackensen			
130th Infantry Regt.	1881	Metz	9
131st Infantry Regt.	1881	Morchingen	9
132nd Infantry Regt.	1881	Strassburg i.E.	9
133rd Infantry Regt.	1881	Zwickau	26

134th Infantry Regt.	1881	Plauen	26
135th Infantry Regt.	1882	Diedenbosen	9
136th Infantry Regt.	1887	Strassburg i.E.	9
137th Infantry Regt.	1887	Hagenau	9
138th Infantry Regt.	1887	Dieuze	9
139th Infantry Regt.	1887	Dobelin	26
140th Infantry Regt.	1890	Hohenslaza	9
141st Infantry Regt.	1890	Graudenz Strassburg i. W. P.	9
142nd Infantry Regt.	1890	Muhlhausen i. E Muhlhausen i. B	28
143rd Infantry Regt.	1890	Strassburg i.E. Mutzig	9
144th Infantry Regt.	1890	Metz Diedenhofen	9
145th Kings Inf. Regt.	1890	Metz	8a
146th Infantry Regt.	1897	Allenstein	9
147th Infantry Regt. Feldm. v. Hindenburg	1897	Lynk Lotzen	9
148th Infantry Regt.	1897	Elbing Bromberg Braunberg	9
149th Infantry Regt.	1897	Schneidemuhl Otsch, Krone	9
150th Infantry Regt.	1897	Allenstein	9
151st Infantry Regt.	1897	Gensburg Bischofsberg	9
152nd Infantry Regt. German Orders Regiment	1897	Marienburg Stuhm	9
153rd Infantry Regt.	1897	Altenburg Merseburg	9-21
154th Infantry Regt.	1897	Tauer Striegau	9
155th Infantry Regt.	1897	Ostrowo Pleschen	9
156th Infantry Regt.	1897	Beuthen Tarnowitz	9
157th Infantry Regt.	1897	Brieg	9
158th Infantry Regt.	1897	Paderborn Sennelager	9
159th Infantry Regt.	1897	Muhlhausen a/R Geldern	9
160th Infantry Regt.	1897	Bonn, Dietz Euskirchen	9
161st Infantry Regt.	1897	Duren, Julich Cologne, Trier	9
162nd Infantry Regt.	1897	Lubeck Eutin	9
163rd Infantry Regt.	1897	Neumunster Heide, Lockstedt	9

164th Infantry Regt.	1813	Hameln Holzminden	12
165th Infantry Regt.	1813	Quedlinburg Blankenburg	12
166th Infantry Regt.	1897	Bitsch	9
167th Infantry Regt.	1897	Cassel Muhlhausen i. T	9
168th Infantry Regt.	1897	Offenbach Butzbach, Friedberg i. H.	30
169th Infantry Regt	1897	Lahr Villingen	28
170th Infantry Regt.	1897	Offenburg Donauesch	28
171st Infantry Regt.	1897	Colmar i. E	9
172nd Infantry Regt.	1897	Neubreisach	9
173rd Infantry Regt.	1897	St. Avold Metz	9
174th Infantry Regt.	1897	Forbach	9
175th Infantry Regt.	1897	Graudenz, Schwetz	9
176th Infantry Regt.	1897	Kulm Thorn	9
177th Infantry Regt.	1897	Dresden Koenigsbruck	26
178th Infantry Regt.	1897	Kamenz	26
179th Infantry Regt.	1897	Leisberg Wurzen	26
180th Infantry Regt.	1897	Tubingen Gmund	34
181st Infantry Regt.	1887	Chemnitz Zwickau Glauchau	26
182. Infantry Regt.	1912	Freiberg Koenigsbruck	26

Bavarian Army Infantry Regiments

Life Guard Infantry Regt.	1814	Munich	35
1st Infantry Regt. King's Regt.	1778	Munich	36
2nd Infantry Regt. Crown Prince's Regt.	1682	Munich	36
3rd Infantry Regt. Prince Karl of Bavaria	1698	Augsburg	36
4th Infantry Regt. King Wilhelm of Wurttemberg	1706	Metz	36
5th Infantry Regt. Grand Duke Ludwig of Hessen	1722	Bamberg	36

6th Infantry Regt.	1725	Amberg	36
Kaiser Wilhelm, King of Prussia			
7th Infantry Regt.	1732	Bayreuth	36
Prince Leopold			
8th Infantry Regt.	1753	Metz	36
Grand Duke Friedrich of Baden			
9th Infantry Regt.	1803	Wurzburg	36
Wrede			
10th Infantry Regt.	1682	Ingolstadt	36
King's Regt.			
11th Infantry Regt.	1805	Regensburg	36
von der Tann			
12th Infantry Regt.	1814	Neu Ulm	36
Prince Arnulf			
13th Infantry Regt.	1806	Ingolstadt	36
Kaiser Franz Joseph of Austria		Eichstatt	
14th Infantry Regt.	1814	Nuremberg	36
Hartmann			
15th Infantry Regt.	1722	Neuburg/Donau	36
Friedrich August of Saxony			
16th Infantry Regt.	1878	Passau	36
Grand Duke Ferdinand of Toscany		Landshut	
17th Infantry Regt.	1878	Germersheim	36
Orff			
18th Infantry Regt.	1881	Landau	36
Prince Ludwig Fredinand			
19th Infantry Regt.	1890	Erlangen	36
20th Infantry Regt.	1897	Lindau Kempten	36
Prince Franz			
21st Infantry Regt.	1897	Furth Sulzback	36
Grand Duke Fried. Franz. IV		of Mecklen. Schwerin	
22nd Infantry Regt.	1897	Zweibrucken	36
Duke Wilhelm of Hohenzollern		Saargemund	
23rd Infantry Regt.	1897	Landau Germersheim	36
King Ferdinand of Bulgaria			

Appendix C:
Regulations Related to the Evolution of the Spiked Helmet

As noted in Chapter 1, the Model 1842 spiked helmet was to be worn by all regiments of Infantry, Artillery, Jäger, and Schutzen. Dragoon Regiments and Pioneer Battalion enlisted men wore the model 1842 helmet, but with silver metal trim. The chinscales and star retainers for officers remained gold for units that wore silver trim.

1843 Pickelhaube adopted for use by troops of the **Grand Duchy of Oldenburg**.

1843 A.K.O. of 22 February
The **1st Guard Regiment of Foot** will be allowed to change the metal trim of the helmet to German Silver. Officers were allowed to use the six-sided fluted spike. Star retainers for officers and the chinscales used by all ranks remained gold.

1843 A.K.O. of 1 March
Officer of the Pioneer Battalions were ordered to wear the new patterned spike helmet. Metal trim was to be silver except the star retainers for officer and the chinscales used by all ranks which remained gold.

1843 A.K.O. of 5 April
Regiments that were allowed to wear a colored pompom on the old pattern shako are now allowed to wear a **horsehair plume** in place of the spike for parades. Regiments of the Guard and Guard Grenadier Regiments wear white plumes. Fusiliers and Regiment No. 8 wore black plumes. The trumpeters and musicians of the units wore red plumes. The plumes are mounted on the helmet by removal of the spike and replacing

it with a 13 cm. plume holder (trichter) in the shape of an elongated spike. The hair was cut to the level of the upper sewn seam of the front visor.

The 1st Grenadier Regiment was awarded the helmet banner "**1619**" to commemorate the date of its establishment. This stamped metal banner with blackened lettering and was worn below the FWR eagle front plate and above the upper seam of the front visor. Historical research later revealed that the establishment date of 1619 was in error for this regiment. On **November 6, 1888** the banner "**1655**" replaced the "**1619**" banner.

Fusilier Regiment 34 was allowed to add the award banner "*Fur Auszeichnung die vormalig Koenigl. Schwedischen Leibregt. Koenigen*" for recognition of service as the body guard regiment of the Queen of Sweden. The stamped metal banner with blackened lettering and was worn above the eagle front plate. (* The award banner was extended to the enlisted men of the 5th and 6th Companies of the 33rd Regiment on December 5, 1865. On May 19, 1891 officers of these companies were also allowed to wear the special banner)

1844 A.K.O. of 19 September * **MODEL 1844 for Artillery***

Due to the incidence of injury among artillery soldiers wearing the new spike helmet, artillery regiments are instructed to **replace the spike with an elongated ball**. (*By the end of the decade a stylized round ball replaced the elongated ball).

1845 Pickelhaube adopted for use by troops of the following states:

Grand Duchy of Saxe-Weimar
Duchy of Saxe-Altenburg
Principalities of Lippe_Detmold, Reuss and Waldeck
Free (Hansa) Cities of Hamburg and Luebeck

1846 Pickelhaube adopted for use by troops of the following states:

Duchy of Anhalt
Elector of Hessen Kassel
Duchy of Saxe-Meinngen-Hildburghausen
Kingdom of Hannover
Free (Hansa) City of Bremen

1846 A.K.O. of 27 October

The leather cockade was to be replaced by a **wool cockade** for the enlisted man and the **silk cockade** for the officers. (*Within three years the quartermaster mandated the use of metal cockades.)

1847 A.K.O. of 4 March

The A.K.O. of 4 March 1847 established the **Prussian Army Non-Commissioned Officers School**. Staff of the school wear the standard infantry helmet and used as the front plate the heraldic Prussian eagle with the star of the Black Eagle Order on its breast. There was not an officer model of this helmet.

1848 Pickelhaube adopted for use by troops of the following states:

Grand Duchy of Mecklenburg-Schwerin
Grand Duchy of Mecklenburg-Strelitz
Duchies of Lauenburg and Schleswig-Holstein

War Ministry Order March 21, **1848** through 14 March **1851**

In response to the **Revolution of 1848**, the Prussian cockade was replaced with the **Black-Red-Gold cockade of the German Confederation.**

1848 A.K.O. of 1 May

General Officers are ordered to wear the spiked helmet (*Prior to this date the Prussian General Officers still wore the old style feathered hat). The General Officers used as their front plate the Guard Eagle with the enameled star of the Black Eagle Order. The spike will be fluted on six sides. For parade and gala events, the spike will be replaced with a feathered plumed mounted on a six sided fluted trichter. The feathers will be on the outside white and on the inside black.

1848 General Order

Depot and **Train officers** wear the spiked helmet with gold trim, six sided fluted spike and the dragoon style eagle.

1849 Pickelhaube adopted for use by troops of the following states:

Grand Duchy of Baden
Grand Duchy of Hessen-Darmstadt
Duchy of Nassau
Landgrave of Hessen-Homburg

1849 A.K.O. of 3 July

For reasons of camouflage, all units are instructed at the outbreak of hostilities to **paint the bright metal trim with black lacquer**. At the end of hostilities, the black lacquer is to be removed. (*This was done by Prussian troops who participated in the war with Denmark in 1849 and the suppression of the revolution in Baden and the Bavarian Pfalz in 1848-49. The King of Prussia reprimanded the returning troops for not having removed the black paint on their return to Berlin. Due to this, the black paint was no longer used.)

1849 A.K.O. of 18 October

9th Infantry Regiment is awarded the banner "**Colberg 1807**" to commemorate the regiment's service during the War of Liberation against Napoleon Bonaparte. Banner is made of stamped metal with blackened letterings and ward above the head of the eagle front plate.

1850 Pickelhaube adopted for use by troops of the Free City of Frankfurt a. Main

1850 A.K.O. of 17 March

The **Prussian Marine Infantry** sea battalion adopts the spiked helmet. Due to the close quarters of sea duty, the spike is removed and replaced with a ball like the one used by the artillery regiments.

1851 Pickelhaube adopted for use by troops of the following states:

Principality of Schwarzburg-Rudolstadt

Principality of Schwarzburg-Sonderhausen

1853 Pickelhaube adopted for use by troops of the **Duchy of Saxe-Coburg-Gotha**

1854 A.K.O. of 26 January

Enlisted men of the **Train** units adopt the **spiked helmet**. Guard Train Battalion wear the Guard Landwehr eagle with star and reserve cross. Line units carry the heraldic eagle with a white reserve cross on the eagle's breast.

1854 A.K.O. of 14 March

Jaeger and Schutzen units adopt the **leather shako** with flat brass chinscales. The Jaeger commanders complained that the spiked helmet was too large and bulky for their use.

1855 A.K.O. of 5 March

Non-Regimental Army Officers are ordered to wear a white plume for parade dress.

1856 A.K.O. of 26 June

The **chinscales** used by **troops of foot** are changed from their rounded configuration to **the flat form**. The rosette screw fastener is reduced in size to be flush with the shape of the rosette.

1857 A.K.O. of 24 December ***MODEL 1857***

In order to **reduce the overall size and weight of the helmet**, the leather body is reduced in height by approximately 2 cm. Helmets already in service have a wedge shaped piece cut out of the top of the body under the spike and the leather resewn. New issue helmets will reflect the smaller size.

1859 A.K.O. of 16 September

Regiments that were allowed to wear a colored pompom on the old pattern shako are now allowed to wear a **horsehair plume** in place of the spike for parades. Regiments of the Guard and Guard Grenadier Regiments wear white plumes. Fusiliers and Regiment No. 8 wore black plumes. The trumpeters and musicians of the units wore red plumes. The plumes are mounted on the helmet by removal of the spike and replacing it with a 13 cm. plume holder (trichter) in the shape of an elongated spike. The hair was cut to the level of the upper seam of the front visor.

The **Reservist Cross** worn by active duty **Train officers is removed.** Both Guard and Line units now wear active duty helmets. The fluted spike is replaced with a smooth spike. For parade the Guard Train Battalion now wear a white plume.

1860 A.K.O. of 10 May

A new front plate style is introduced. All eagles now carry the banner **"Mit Gott fur Koenig und Vaterland"**. As a cost saving measure old pattern front plates will have a separate banner attached to the eagles breast.

1860 A.K.O. of 4 November ***MODEL 1860***

Further reduction of the size of the helmet is ordered for both officers and enlisted men. For helmets still in service, the front and rear visor are removed. The leather body is cut down approximately 4 cm. at the base. The visors are then resewn onto the leather body and the holes for the front plate and chinscales are repositioned. For new issue helmets of Model 1860, the cross spike base configuration is changed with the front extension reduced in size to allow for a properly sized front plate. The base now measures 17 cm side to side and 14 cm front to back. The height of the spike and throat is reduced to 10 cm. .

With reduction of helmet and front plate size, award banners for Regiments 9 and 34 are moved to a position on the upper legs of the eagle.

1861 A.K.O. of 16 March

Due to the reduction of the helmet size in 1860 the plumes worn for parade now reach to the bottom of the helmet front visor. The **plume trichters are lengthened by 4 cm**. to return the plume edge to the top seam of the front visor.

The banner "Mit Gott fur Koenig und Vaterland" added to the front plate. For reason of cost containment, a stamped ribbon will be added to all front plates then in service. All front plates made after this date will have the banner stamped into the face.

1862 A.K.O. of 6 February

Marine Infantry Sea Battalion adopts **the shako**. The leather body is covered with blue felt. The front plate has an eagle atop an anchor.

1863 Directive of the War Ministry 27 January

Enlisted men of the **Train Battalion** adopt the **shako**. Officers retain the spiked helmet.

1867 Pickelhaube adopted for use by troops of the **Kingdom of Saxony**

1867 A.K.O. of 16 March ***MODEL 1867***

A radically different **helmet model for enlisted men of the foot** troops is introduced. The front visor is now round with a metal edging. The body size is now reduced to 14 cm. The crossed spike base is replaced with a round base with a 9.5 cm. spike and throat. The cockade is reduced in size from 6.5 cm. to 5.5 cm.. The back spine is completely eliminated.

1867 A.K.O. of 3 April

Officers of the **Train** adopt the new helmet model with 4 star retainers. The chinscales remain rounded.

1867 A.K.O. of 2 May

Officers of the foot troops **adopt** the new **helmet model** with 4 star retainers. Non-Regimental Officers retained the Model 1860 helmet with Prussian Line eagle and rounded chinscales. All metal trim is in gold.

1868 Military Convention of 20 June

In accordance with the Military Convention of 1867 allied state regiments were added to the Prussian Army. They included:

Anhalt (IR 93)
Grand Ducal Saxe Weimar (IR 94)
Ducal Saxe Thuringian (IR 95, *96-I Bat. and later 153-III Bat.)
Reuss (IR 96-II Bat.)
Schwarzburg Rudolstadt (IR 96-III Bat.)
*the IR 96-I Bat. wore the Prussian Line eagle after Apr. 1, 1897.

Each regiment wore the heraldic Prussian eagle with the banner "Mit Gott fur Fuerst und Vaterland". The eagle was mounted with a silver star and the crest of the individual allied state.

1869 Pickelhaube adopted for use by troops of the **Kingdom of Wuerttemberg**

1870 A.K.O. of 3 March

In accordance with the Military Convention of 1867 the state of Oldenburg (IR 91) is added to the Prussian Army. This regiment wore the heraldic Prussian eagle (with "Mit Gott fur Koenig und Vaterland" banner) on which was mounted a silver star and the crest of Oldenburg.

1871 A.K.O. of 23 November ***MODEL 1871***

Helmet Model 1867 without the back spine proves unstable. To improve stability, a **metal back spine is returned to the helmet**. On this date, the new style pin backed rosette is adopted by the officer.

*the IR 96-I Bat. wore the Prussian Line eagle after Apr. 1, 1897

1871 Grand Ducal (Hessen Darmstadt) Order of the Day 5 December

Life Guard Infantry Regt. No. 115 awarded the banner "1621" to commemorate the date the unit was founded. Banner made of stamped brass with blackened numbers to be worn above the helmet front plate. All metal trim in gold with rounded chinscales.

1872 Grand Ducal (Hessen Darmstadt) Order of the Day 1 January

Pioneer Company (9th Company) 117th Inf. Reg. awarded the **crossed pick and axe over an anchor** to be worn on the helmet front plate. All metal trim in gold.

1871 Allerhoechste Muendliche Befehl (Royal Oral Declaration) of 1 March
Officers of the 7th Grenadier Regiment received the monogram of Kaiser Wilhelm I for use as the chinscale rosette and on their dagger.

1882 Directive of the War Ministry of 9 February
Foot Artillery Regiments now adopt flat styled chinscales. The length of the plume is adjusted to conform to the style of the troops of foot.

1884 A.K.O. of 8 May
For identification during maneuvers, a **white cloth cover** is introduced to cover the helmet body. The spike protrudes through the top while the bottom extends to the top of the helmet visor.

1886 Military Convention of March 18
In accordance with the Military Convention of 1886, the **Duchy of Braunschweig** placed its regiment with the Prussian Army as the 92nd Infantry Regiment. The helmet front late was the heraldic Prussian eagle with the banner "Mit Gott fur Fuerst und Vaterland". The eagle was mounted with the silver Star of the House Order of Braunschweig over the banner "**Peninsula**". The officer star was decorated with colored enamel.
*see AKO March 30, 1889

1886 Bavarian War Ministry Decree of 10 September
The spiked helmet is adopted for use by troops of the **Bavarian Army**. Helmet has a black lacquered leather body similar to the Prussian dragoon design. The Bavarian style front plate was 18 cm wide and 13 cm tall. Flat (rounded for mounted units) scaled chinstraps in the Prussian style were affixed to the helmet body with a rosette. The stamped metal non-serrated Bavarian (silver & light blue) cockade was worn on the right side of the helmet.

Officers wore the same style helmet with gilded metal trim and a matt fire gilded front plate. Spike base was ornamented with a "pearl and diamond" ring and affixed to the helmet body with 3 six sided star retainers (the front leg of the spike base overlapped by the front plate). Chinscales were flat (rounded for mounted units) and affixed to the helmet body with a split leg rosette.

Infantry, Cavalry, Train, Artillery (with spike), and Jäger units wore the same pattern of spiked helmet.

1887 A.K.O. of 3 March ***MODEL 1887***

Again **a new helmet style for enlisted men of the troops of foot** is introduced. The metal front visor trim is removed. The new styled front visor has a hardened beaded edge. The pearl ring at the base of the spike throat is removed in favor of a simple rolled seam. The screw type rosette and chinscales are removed and replaced with leather strap hung on a brass hook. The cockade is attached under the hook to the helmet body. Guard and Grenadiers Regiments retain chinscales with attachments to lock onto the hook retainers. Officers retain the Model 1871 helmet. (*A number of Model 1871 helmets were refitted with the Model 1887 chinstrap while retaining the metal edged front visor.)

1888 A.K.O. of 11 November

Award banner for the 1st Grenadier Regiment is changed from "**1619**" to "**1655**" in accordance with newly researched historical archives.

4th Grenadier Regiment is awarded the banner "**1626**" to commemorate the year when it was established. Banner is made of stamped metal with blackened lettering and is worn above the head of the eagle front plate.

1889 A.K.O. of 27 January

1st Guard Regiment 3rd and 4th Companies are awarded the banner "**Semper Talis**" for their past service as the traveling guard of King Friedrich Wilhelm I (this also worn on the Miter helmet). Later in the summer of 1889 the award was extended to the entire 1st Battalion and Regiment Staff.

1889 A.K.O of 30 March

92nd Infantry Regiment (Braunschweig) replaces the House Order Star decoration of the III (Leib) Battalion with a silver Skull and crossed bones over the banner "**Peninsula**".

* see A.K.O. of January 27, 1912

1889 A.K.O. of 28 August

Guard Grenadier Regiments are awarded the Guards Eagle with Star as their helmet front plate.

**Line Grenadier Regiments 1 through 12 begin replacing the FWR eagle front plate with the old style grenadier eagle (guard eagle without star). Changes occurs on the following dates:

March 22 1897 - Grenadier Regiment 7
May 4, 1897 – Grenadier Regiment 2
June 15, 1898 – Grenadier Regiment 8
May 6, 1900 – Grenadier Regiment 1
September 9, 1901 – Grenadier Regiment 3
May 1, 1911 – Grenadier Regiment 4
June 16, 1911 – Grenadier Regiments 5, 9, 10 & 12
August 26, 1913 – Grenadier Regiment 6
August 28, 1913 – Grenadier Regiment 11

1891 A.K.O. of 17 May ***MODEL 1891***

The helmet Model 1887 proved to be unsuccessful. **A new helmet style is introduced for enlisted men** to correct the instability of the Mod. 87. The rounded front visor with metal trim is restored. The hook retainer is replaced with a brass lug (termed the M91 side lug) for the fitting of the chinstrap. Guard and Grenadier Regiments wear flat chinscales fitted over the Model 1891 side lug. The cockade fits over the lug and behind the leather chinstrap buckle.

1891, KMR Nr. 17509 (Bavarian War Ministry Directive) of October 20

For Bavarian enlisted pattern helmets, a leather chinstrap and hook retainer in the style of the Prussian M91 side lug was introduced. Aluminum bronze flat chinscales were used for parade. Cockade was made to fit over M91 side lug.

1892 A.K.O. of 17 May

The **Maneuver/Field Cover** is introduced for use by all troops. The cover is made of rush green cloth and fits over the entire helmet.

1894 A.K.O. of 18 May ***MODEL 1894 for mounted EM***

Introduction of **Model 1891 style for mounted troops**. Rounded chinscales are made to fit over the Model 1891 side lug.

1895 A.K.O. of 25 May ***MODEL 1895 for Enlisted Men troops of foot***

To further **reduce the weight of the helmet** the brass metal trim is now changed to cupro-aluminium. The spike base now has 5 ventilation holes instead of 2. The back spine is fitted with a slide covered ventilation system*. The helmet body is now approximately 12.5 cm. tall. The enlisted mans plume trichter is changed in design from the elongated spike to a round tube (nadel).

*Mounted troops such as Train and Field Artillery keep non-vented back spine until 1904.

1896 Quartermaster Directive

Officer's parade plumes will now be made of buffalo hair. Enlisted plumes remain horse hair.

1896 KMOVBI Nr. 21 (Bavarian Army Order) of 23 July

New helmet style for Bavarian enlisted foot troops similar to the Prussian Model 1891 introduced. Helmet body was made of pressed black lacquered leather. The metal trimmed leather front visor was now rounded. The non-ornamented round spike base had five ventilation holes. Helmet spike is now smooth. Back spine also had a ventilation sleeve. The smaller front plate (11 cm wide and 9 cm tall) was made of tombak or German silver and affixed to the helmet with two loops. Chinstrap (chinscales for parade) continued to use the M91 side lug. Artillery and mounted units continue to wear the M1886 helmet.

Officer model helmets retained the M1886 pattern helmet. Changes include reduction in size of the front plate with the top reaching to the edge of the front leg of the spike base.

* *It was a common practice for the Bavarian Quartermaster Corp to refit the previously issued M1886 for the new M1896 style. Many early M1896 enlisted pattern helmets will have plugged holes for the old pattern cross spike base and a newly sewn round front visor. Some also were refit M1868 Raupenhelm bodies.*

1897 A.K.O. of 28 January 1897

The use of the green field cover made the identification of units in a combat line difficult. In order to alleviate this problem, **regimental identification numbers in red cloth** are placed on the front of each cover.

Line Regiments_______Red. Regt. Number
Reserve Regiments.___Latin "**R**" above Regt. Number
Landwehr Regiments__Latin "**R**" above the Regt. No.
Landsturm Regts._____Red Landwehr Cross

Numbered covers were **not** worn by the Prussian Guard, Grenadier Regt. 89, Grenadier Regt. 109, or the Bavarian Leib Infantry Regt..

On Feb. 2 1900 the Landwehr Regiments replaced the "**L**" with the letter "**R**" on the field cover.

The field cover was worn during field exercises and maneuvers. An **all white field cover** was ordered for maneuver/war games judges by the **A.K.O. of 28 August 1901**. In order to eliminate confusion during the Kaiser Maneuvers of 1908 (**A.K.O. of 19 March 1908**) a **red band** was added to the field cover. This band identified the "red" army during the field exercises. On June 23, 1909 the use of the "maneuver Band" was extended to the entire army.

In the first days of World War I it became apparent that the red numbered cover gave the enemy easy front line intelligence. On **August 15, 1914 the red numbers were replaced with <u>dark green</u> <u>cloth</u>**. In many cases the red numbers were removed and the replacement done with dyes or ink.

By the end of 1914 many Regiments removed the numbers. A Regimental Order of the 91st Reserve Infantry Regt. of December 3, 1914 placed the green numbers on the back of the helmet cover. On **October 27, 1916 all numbers were removed** from the field cover with the exception of the cross for the Landsturm Regiments.

<u>**1897** A.K.O. of 22 March ***MODEL 1897***</u>
To celebrate the 100th anniversary of the birth of Kaiser Wilhem I the combined military services introduce the **Reich's cockade**. The **Black-White-Red cockade** is worn on the right side of the helmet. The **state cockade** is worn on the left side. All helmets from this time on will carry two cockades.

The 7th Grenadier Regiment was awarded a new front plate. This new front plate was the old style (guards regiment eagle without star) eagle with the banner "22 Marz 1797". The banner had blackened lettering and was worn above the eagle's legs on the front plate.

<u>**1897** A.K.O. of 28 May</u>
Non-Regimental Army Officers adopt the Model 1897 officer's helmet. Metal trim is gold with rounded front visor, round spike base and rounded chinscales.

<u>**1897** Grand Ducal (Hessen Darmstadt) Oral Decree Fall 1897</u>
As is the custom for Life Guard Regiments of the other German states, the Life Guar Infantry Regiment is ordered to change the metal trim of the helmet to a silver color in

time for the fall maneuvers to be viewed by Kaiser Wilhelm II. For reasons of economy, helmets in service are washed with a mercury silver solution to bleach the existing brass trim. Unfortunately the bleaching technique does not last and causes the trim to turn to a gray like color.

1897 Grand Ducal (Hessen Darmstadt) Order of the Day of 25 November

In response to the failed attempt at bleaching the helmet trim, Life Guard Infantry Regt. No 115 receives new helmet with all metal trim in silver. Front plate with double wreathed Lion centered with the house order star of the Ludwigs-Orden. Star for officers in has colored enamel center. Other ranks have stamped metal star. The banner "1621" is located above the front plate. Chinscales are now to be flat.

1900 A.K.O. of 6 May

1st Grenadier Regiment replaced the FWR eagle with the old style grenadier eagle (guard eagle without star). The banner "**1655**" is placed on the front of the eagle above the legs.

1903 A.K.O. of 25 May

Enlisted men of the **Train Battalions** now return to wearing the **spiked helmet**. Rounded chinscales are worn over the Model 1891 side lug.

1911 A.K.O. of 1 May

4th Grenadier Regiment replaced the FWR eagle with the old style grenadier eagle (guard eagle without star). The banner "**1626**" remains above the eagles head.

1912 A.K.O. of 27 January

92nd Infantry Regiment (Braunschweig) replaces the House Order Star* worn by the I and II battalions with the silver Skull and crossed bones atop the banner "**Peninsula**" as already used by the III battalion.

*Landwehr District Officers continue to wear the House Order Star with Reserve front plate and cross on their helmets until end of WWI.

1913 KMVOBI No. 14 (Bavarian War Ministry Order) of 13 April 1913

New helmet decoration for General Officers. The center shield of the helmet front plate will be decorated with colored enamel. KMVOBI No. 6 of February 20, 1914 extends the front plate to all officers in the General a la Suite and in General Officer staff

1913 A.K.O. of 16 June

9th Grenadier Regiment replaced the FWR eagle with the old style grenadier eagle (guard eagle without star). The banner "**Colberg 1807**" is placed on the front of the eagle above the legs.

1914 KME 4149 (Bavarian War Ministry Regulation) of 17 February

Chinscales for all units (Foot and mounted troops alike) are changed to the rounded form. This order applies to enlisted and officer pattern helmets. Chinscaled straps for parade are no longer to be worn by enlisted foot units (with the exception of Foot Artillery).

1915 A.K.O. of 21 September ***MODEL 1915***

The extreme demands of the Great War leads to the development of the **"War Model" spiked helmet**. The Model 1895 helmet retains the same leather body with the replacement of bright metal trim (gold and silver) with a matte gray painted or chemically oxidized steel trim The spike (or ball) is made to be removable at the base of the throat by a bayonet lock mechanism. Other German states follow the Prussian lead by adopting the Model 1915 helmet. Württemberg on October 10, 1915, Saxony on November 9, 1915, and Bavaria on November 1, 1915.

1916 (KMVOBI Nr. 17) (Bavarian War Ministry Regulation) of 6 April

Bavarian Artillery Regiments which formerly wore a standard spike top now adopt the "ball" ornament.

The introduction of the **Model 1916** "coal scuttle" steel helmet rapidly replaced the spiked helmet in the field. The spiked helmet was worn throughout the war era by rear echelon troops, and for home service in Germany. Manufacturers of officer helmets also adopted some of the Model 1915 modifications. Officer style spikes are made to be removable at the base, and Model 1891 side lugs are used to allow the officer to remove the chinscales in the field and replace it with a leather chinstrap. Even after WWI many "Old Guard" officers continued to wear the spiked helmet, even during the Weimar era.

Appendix D:
Pioneer Battalions

Frontplate numbers on pages 30-31

Battalino	**Est.**	**Hdq.**	**Frontplate**
Guard Pioneer Bat.	1810	Berlin	3
1st Pioneer Battalion Prince Radziwill	1780	Koenigsberg i/P	4(S)*
2nd Pioneer Battalion	1816	Stettin	9(S)
3rd Pioneer Battalion von Rauch	1741	Spandau	4(S)
4th Pioneer Battalion	1816	Magdeburg	9(S)
5th Pioneer Battalion	1816	Glogau	9(S)
6th Pioneer Battalion	1816	Neisse	9(S)
7th Pioneer Battalion	1816	Cologne	9(S)
8th Pioneer Battalion	1816	Koblenz	9(S)
9th Pioneer Battalion	1866	Harburg	9(S)
10th Pioneer Battalion	1804	Minden	11(S)
11th Pioneer Battalion	1842	Hannover	9(S)

Minden

12th Pioneer Battalion	1698	Pirna	25
13th Pioneer Battalion	1817	Ulm	33
14th Pioneer Battalion	1850	Kehl	28(S)
15th Pioneer Battalion	1871	Strassburg i. E.	9(S)
16th Pioneer Battalion	1881	Metz	9(S)
19th Pioneer Battalion	1893	Strassburg i. E.	9(S)
20th Pioneer Battalion	1893	Metz	9(S)
21st Pioneer Battalion	1901	Mainz	9(S)
22nd Pioneer Battalion	1899	Kiessa	25
23rd Pioneer Battalion	1907	Graudenz	9(S)
24th Pioneer Battalion	1908	Cologne	9(S)
25th Pioneer Battalion	1909	Mainz	9(S)
26th Pioneer Battalion	1912	Graudenz	9(S)
27th Pioneer Battalion	1912	Trier	9(S)
28th Pioneer Battalion	1913	Kustrin	9(S)
29th Pioneer Battalion	1913	Posen	9(S)
30th Pioneer Battalion	1913	Ehrenbreitstein	9(S)

*(S) indicates Silver Metal color for front plate

Bavarian Army Pioneer Battalions

1st Pioneer Battalion	1900	Munich	35
2nd Pioneer Battalion	1872	Speyer	35
3rd Pioneer Battalion	1872	Ingolstadt	35
4th Pioneer Battalion	1912	Ingolstadt	35

List of Contributors

The authors gratefully acknowledge the following individuals who contributed photographs from their collections and information from their research libraries:

Rich Ames
Art Allen
Paul Boyer
Tony Cowan
Harry Fakner
Walter Hartmann
Wolf Albrecht Kainz
Chip Minx
Jim Runyon
John Sandidge
Remy Schaal
Wm. Randall Trawnik
Charles Van Hoenacker

The Research Library / Wehrgeschichtlichesmuseum Rastatt

Bibliography

Museums
Bayerische Armee Museum, Ingolstadt, Germany
Fort de la Pompelle, Reims, France
Kavallerie Museum Vornholz, Schloss, Ostenfelde im Westfallen, Germany
Wehrgeschichtliches Museum, Schloss, Rastatt, Germany

Sources

Henckel, Carl. *ATLAS DES DEUTSCHEN REICHSHEERES*, 1902, reprint J.H. Bielitz & W. Eger, Wallertheim, 1984.

Hermann, Rainer: *MILITAERISCHE KOPFBEDECKUNGEN der KAISERZEIT*, Motorbuch Verlag, Stuttgart, 1999.

Kraus, Juergen, *DIE FELDGRAUE UNIFORMIERGUNG des DEUTSCHEN HEEREN 1907-1918 Bande I- II*, Motorbuch Verlag, Stuttgart, 2000.

Kube, Jan, *MILITARIA-HELMETS and UNIFORMS 1729-1918*, Schiffer Military History, West Chester, 1990.

Laine, Didier, *L'ARMEE ALLEMANDE en 1914*, Chromos Service, Paris, 1984
Laine, Didier, *LA REPERTOIRE de L'ARMEE ALLEMANDE 1914*, Diffusions Histoire, Chennevieres, 1998.

Larcarde, Jean-Louis, *CASQUES' a POINTE 1842-1918 – TROUPES a PIED*, Jacques Granchier, Paris, 1983.

Mueller, Heinrich, *EUROPAEISCHE HELME*, Verlag der DDR, Berlin 1971.

Pietsche, Paul, *DIE FORMATIONS und UNIFORMIERUNGS GESCHICHTE des PREUSSISCHEN HEERES 1908-1914 Bande I-II*, Verlag Gerhard Schulz, Hamburg 1966.

Pietsche, Paul, et al., *DAS DEUTSCHE HEERE Band I-II-III*, W. Spemann Verlag, Stuttgart, 1982.

Sanders, Paul, *HEAD DRESS of IMPERIAL GERMANY 1880-1918*, Schiffer Military History, Atglen, Pa. 2001.

Seibold, Walter; Schulz, Gerd, *DIE HELME DER KOENIGLICH BAYERISCHEN ARMEE 1806-1918,* Bayrische Militaerverlag G.M. Schulz, Groebenzell, 1999.

Schiers, Ulrich, DEUTSCHE HELME 1897-1914, Graf Klenau Verlag GmbH, Fridingen, 1978.

Wannewetsch, Walter, *KOENIGREICH WUERTTEMBERG-KOPFBEDECKUNGEN 1869-1919*, Steinach Verlag, Stuttgart, 1993.